PREFACE

I am delighted to share with you the story behind "Survival Food: South African Pioneer Cuisine." This book is not just a collection of recipes; it's a journey through history, a celebration of heritage, and a testament to the enduring power of food to unite us all

My adventure into the world of South African pioneer cuisine began when I moved to the United States in 2017 after marrying John B Wells. At that time, my cooking repertoire consisted mainly of the flavors and techniques I learned from my mother and grandmother in South Africa. Little did I know that these flavors would captivate John B's taste buds so profoundly that he encouraged me to share our culinary heritage with the world.

The decision to write this book was born out of a deep love for the delicious food of South Africa and a desire to unravel the rich tapestry of our people's history. What struck me the most while compiling these recipes was the realization that, at our core, we share more in common than we might think. We are all part of the same human family; we merely embarked on different journeys that brought us to different shores.

"Pioneer Boere Recipes" were more than just meals; they were the cornerstone of survival for the intrepid Boere settlers who embarked on ventures like the Great Trek in South Africa between 1835 and 1854. These pioneers faced countless challenges and uncertainties along their path, but they possessed the remarkable resourcefulness and ingenuity to sustain themselves and their families.

With limited access to markets and provisions, they crafted recipes using locally sourced produce, game meat, and preserved goods. These recipes were not just delicious; they were designed to provide nourishment, sustenance, and comfort during difficult times. Dishes like potjiekos, biltong, and melktert were born out of necessity and practicality, yet they have evolved into beloved culinary treasures that continue to enrich South African culture today.

These recipes also fostered a sense of community and resilience among the settlers. Passed down through generations, they preserve our culinary heritage and connect us to our pioneering roots. In times of plenty, they remind us of the pioneers' perseverance, and in times of scarcity, they serve as a lifeline, ensuring that families have access to nourishing meals even during challenging periods.

Today, Pioneer Boere Recipes offer a link to our rich history, reminding us of the strength and resourcefulness of those who came before us. They continue to be cherished as culinary treasures, providing not only delicious meals but also a connection to our past and a sense of security for our families, both in good times and in bad. May the recipes within these pages inspire you to create your own wonderful memories and celebrate the enduring spirit of our shared human journey.

With warm wishes and blessings,
Brendi Wells

FOREWORD

It is with great pleasure and excitement that I introduce you to "Survival Food: South African Pioneer Cuisine," a culinary journey that holds a special place in my heart. Having had the privilege of being married to Brendi, whose South African roots run deep, I've had the incredible opportunity to savor the rich and diverse flavors of South African cuisine.

From the moment I first tasted Brendi's homemade dishes, I was hooked. Her cooking not only delighted my taste buds but also transported me to a world of tradition, history, and culture that was entirely new to me. I was captivated by the aromas that wafted from our kitchen and the stories behind each dish, passed down through generations of South African cooks.

It was this fascination that led me to encourage Brendi to share her culinary expertise with the world. I couldn't help but feel that others should have the chance to experience the incredible flavors and heartwarming stories that I had come to cherish. And so, "Survival Food" was born.

As I witnessed the dedication and passion that Brendi poured into this cookbook, I was continually amazed by the result. It's not just a collection of recipes; it's a window into a world where food is more than sustenance—it's a celebration of life, history, and shared moments with loved ones.

With each turn of the page, you'll embark on a culinary adventure that not only tantalizes your taste buds but also connects you to a vibrant South African culture that is steeped in tradition and diversity. The recipes within these pages are a testament to the love and care that go into South African cooking, and they reflect the beautiful tapestry of flavors that make it truly unique.

I am thrilled to see Brendi's passion and talent come to life in this book, and I have no doubt that it will inspire you to create your own unforgettable South African food experiences. Whether you're a seasoned chef or a beginner in the kitchen, these recipes are designed to bring the warmth and flavors of South Africa to your table.

So, without further ado, I invite you to embark on this culinary journey, explore the recipes, and savor the stories that have been lovingly crafted within these pages. May "Survival Food" bring a taste of South Africa to your home and fill your hearts with the same joy and wonder that it has brought to mine.

With heartfelt enthusiasm,
John B Wells

FOREWORD

You are holding in your hands one of the most interesting books I have read. The mix of a concise history of the Boer peoples and their survival foods are an inspiration to behold.

Reading this book has made me aware of the trials and tribulations of these hardy and brave pioneers, the Afrikaners, who, with relentless perseverance while dealing with the dangerous and hostile forces, tamed the land. The pioneers and their everyday experiences along with military exploits and battles are impressively told as the reader is introduced to the heroic men and women who forged their own nation.

The book should firmly stand as a further inspiration for any group or culture that would seek to establish their own rights against seemingly impossible odds while building an ever-lasting society.

And the food! The food made with an indelible passion to survive as an underlying reality should satisfy the culinary appetites of anyone.

Brendi Wells has created a significant addition to any and all global communities that also have to deal with their own daily life and futures.

Now, if you will permit me, I must partake of my marvelously delicious coriander biltong delights while I listen to the strains of Wys My Die Plek.

Hanshi Stephen Kaufman

FOREWORD

We all have cherished memories of gathering with friends and loved ones, and these memories can evoke a myriad of emotions. Whether those gatherings were grand celebrations or intimate moments, they revolved around a table filled with delectable dishes, prepared with love. Such special occasions not only involve a delightful feast but also etch a timeless image in our minds—one we can recall vividly. As you reminisce about the purpose of each occasion, your mind's eye conjures up the banquet spread before you, the enticing aroma of lovingly prepared food, and yes, even the emotions stirred by those memories.

These moments are truly special, and each of us can recollect the distinct flavors and aromas that marked our unique experiences. Despite the variations in tastes and scents, it's crucial to remember that what we encountered in those differences were the intimate thoughts and intentions of cooks from diverse cultures. In your hands, Brendi offers you more than just a cookbook; it's a cultural journey. These South African recipes not only allow you to embrace your own traditions but also create a treasure trove of memories to lovingly share with others, no matter where you are.

A cookbook is more than just a collection of recipes; it encapsulates the special times we share with one another. Brendi is deeply passionate about preserving the culture and traditions that bring about joyous memories. These delightful South African recipes will undoubtedly help you craft moments that are filled with love and leave you with lasting memories.

Dr. John Waterman, ND

Survival Food: South African Pioneer History and Cuisine

Author: Brendi Wells
Editor: Jeanne Barnard
Design: Marnus Nagel

A Journey to the Heart of South Africa:
The Afrikaner Pioneer's Culinary Expedition

From Roaring Campfires to Beloved Comfort Foods:
A Tale of Resilience, Resourcefulness, and Reverence for the Land.

Long ago, in the heart of the untamed South African wilderness,
thousands of South African families embarked on the "Groot Trek",
in search of freedom and a new way of life. This group of people,
known as the "Voortrekkers" or Pioneers, travelled across
the vast savannah with the goal to break away from British control
and create independent territories where they could govern themselves
according to their own cultural, religious, and social values.
They were determined to succeed no matter what challenges lay ahead.

As they journeyed through the rugged terrain, the Pioneers relied
on their culinary skills to keep them fed and nourished.
They built roaring campfires each night and cooked hearty
stews in cast iron pots over the flames. They baked delicious
potbrood and dried fruits to preserve for later.

As they foraged for food and hunted game, the Pioneers
developed a deep appreciation for the natural resources
available to them. They learned to identify the most nutritious plants
for gathering and the most efficient ways to hunt for food.

They developed a strong connection to the land and a respect
for the animals they hunted. Through their ingenuity and perseverance,
the Afrikaner Pioneers were able to establish a thriving settlement
in the heart of the wilderness. They passed down their culinary
traditions and survival skills to future generations, and
these traditions continue to be celebrated and enjoyed today.

The South African's strong heritage and connection to the land
is reflected in the traditional dishes they have developed over the years.
Biltong, a type of dried meat, is still a staple of the South African diet,
and is made by preserving strips of beef or game with salt and spices.
Potbrood is still baked in cast iron pots over open fires,
and is a beloved comfort food across South Africa.

Through their love of food and their connection to the land,
the South African people have created a
culinary tradition that is as rich and diverse as
the South African landscape itself.

Recipe Index

Recipe Index

Stories Index

Measurement Conversions

Converting Ounces to Grams

Ounces	Grams
½	15
1	30
2	60
3	90
4	110
5	140
6	170
7	200
8	225
9	255
10	280
11	310
12	340
13	370
14	400
15	425
16 / 1 Pound	450

Baking Conversions:

Measurement	Equivalent
1 teaspoon	5 ml
1 tablespoon	3 teaspoons / 15 ml
2 tablespoons	1 ounce / 30 ml
4 tablespoons	1/4 cup / 60 ml
5 tablespoons + 1 teaspoon	1/3 cup / 80 ml
1/2 cup	8 tablespoons / 120 ml
1 cup	16 tablespoons / 240 ml
1 quart	2 pints / 4 cups
1 gallon	4 quarts / 16 cups
1 stick butter	8 tablespoons / 1/2 cup / 4 ounces / 113 grams

Conversion Table: Grams to Milliliters (ml) and Ounces (oz)

Grams (g)	Milliliters (ml)	Ounces (oz)	Cups
1 g	1 ml	0.035 oz	-
25 g	25 ml	0.88 oz	-
50 g	50 ml	1.76 oz	-
75 g	75 ml	2.65 oz	-
100 g	100 ml	3.53 oz	-
125 g	125 ml	4.41 oz	-
150 g	150 ml	5.29 oz	-
175 g	175 ml	6.17 oz	-
200 g	200 ml	7.05 oz	-
225 g	225 ml	7.94 oz	-
250 g	250 ml	8.82 oz	1 cup
275 g	275 ml	9.70 oz	-
300 g	300 ml	10.58 oz	-
325 g	325 ml	11.46 oz	-
350 g	350 ml	12.35 oz	-
375 g	375 ml	13.23 oz	-
400 g	400 ml	14.11 oz	-
425 g	425 ml	14.99 oz	-
450 g	450 ml	15.87 oz	2 cups
475 g	475 ml	16.76 oz	-
500 g	500 ml	17.64 oz	-

Converting Gallons, Quarts, Pints, Cups, Ounces, Tablespoons, and Teaspoons:

Measurement	Quarts	Pints	Cups	Ounces	Tablespoons	Teaspoons	Milliliters	Liters
1 gallon	4	8	16	128	-	-	-	3.8
1 quart	-	2	4	32	-	-	950	-
1 pint	-	-	2	16	-	-	480	-
1 cup	-	-	-	-	16	-	240	-
1 ounce	-	-	-	-	2	-	30	-
1 tablespoon	-	-	-	-	-	3	15	-
1 teaspoon	-	-	-	-	-	-	5	-

Measurement Conversions

Conversion	Metric to Imperial	Imperial to Metric
Volume Conversions		
Teaspoons (tsp)	5 ml	1 teaspoon
Tablespoons (tbsp)	15 ml	1 tablespoon
Cups	240 ml	1 cup
Fluid Ounces (fl oz)	30 ml	1 fluid ounce
Milliliters (ml)		
1 teaspoon	0.17 teaspoon (imperial)	5 ml
1 tablespoon	0.33 tablespoon (imperial)	15 ml
1 cup	0.42 cups (imperial)	240 ml
1 fluid ounce	0.03 fluid ounces	30 ml
Weight Conversions		
Ounces (oz)	28 grams	1 ounce
Pounds (lb)	454 grams	1 pound
Grams (g)		
1 ounce	0.035 ounces	28 grams
1 pound	16 ounces	454 grams
Ingredient Specific		
Butter		
Sticks	1 stick = 113 grams	1 stick = 8 tablespoons
Cups	1 cup = 227 grams	1 cup = 16 tablespoons
Flour		
Cups	1 cup = 128 grams	1 cup = 4.5 ounces
Sugar		
Cups	1 cup = 200 grams	1 cup = 7 ounces
Baking Powder		
Teaspoons	1 teaspoon = 5 grams	1 teaspoon
Baking Soda		
Teaspoons	1 teaspoon = 5 grams	1 teaspoon
Yeast		
Teaspoons	1 teaspoon = 3 grams	1 teaspoon

Dry Ingredients:

Imperial (US)	Metric
1 cup	240 ml
1/2 cup	120 ml
1/3 cup	80 ml
1/4 cup	60 ml
1 tablespoon	15 ml
1 teaspoon	5 ml
1 ounce	28 grams
1 pound	454 grams

Wet Ingredients:

Imperial (US)	Metric
1 cup	240 ml
1/2 cup	120 ml
1/3 cup	80 ml
1/4 cup	60 ml
1 tablespoon	15 ml
1 teaspoon	5 ml
1 fluid ounce	30 ml
1 pint	480 ml
1 quart	950 ml
1 gallon	3.8 liters

Fahrenheit (°F)	Celsius (°C)
176°F	80°C
212°F	100°C
230°F	110°C
248°F	120°C
284°F	140°C
320°F	160°C
356°F	180°C
392°F	200°C
410°F	210°C
428°F	220°C
464°F	240°C
500°F	260°C

Freezing & Storage

Comprehensive List of Foods for Freezing and Maximum Storage Duration

Food	Preparation	Max Freezing Duration
Soups and Stews	Cook and cool	2-3 months
Casseroles & One-Pot Meals	Assemble and cook	2-3 months
Chili	Cook and cool	3-4 months
Meat (cooked)	Cook and cool	2-3 months
Poultry (cooked)	Cook and cool	2-3 months
Seafood (cooked)	Cook and cool	2-3 months
Rice & Grain Dishes (cooked)	Cook and cool	2-3 months
Pasta (cooked)	Cook and cool	2-3 months
Pizza	Assemble and bake	1-2 months
Bread & Baked Goods	Bake and cool	2-3 months
Cookies & Cookie Dough	Prepare and chill	3-6 months
Cakes & Cupcakes	Bake and cool	2-3 months
Muffins & Quick Breads	Bake and cool	2-3 months
Pancakes & Waffles	Cook and cool	2-3 months
Pie & Pastry	Bake and cool	2-3 months
Fruit & Vegetable Purees	Cook, puree, and cool	8-12 months (varies by type)
Vegetables	Blanch and cool	8-12 months (varies by type)
Fruits (sliced or whole)	Freeze on a tray, then store	8-12 months (varies by type)
Berries	Freeze on a tray, then store	8-12 months (varies by type)
Smoothie Packs	Prepare and freeze in bags	2-3 months
Sauces & Gravies	Cook and cool	2-3 months
Homemade Stocks & Broths	Cook and cool	2-3 months
Herbs (chopped in oil /butter)	Freeze in ice cube trays	6-12 months

Remember to use proper freezer-safe containers or resealable bags, remove excess air to prevent freezer burn, and label each item with the name and date of freezing. These storage durations are general guidelines, and it's essential to use your judgment and discretion when consuming frozen foods.

Always ensure food safety practices for the best results.

FAMOUS BILTONG

Proudly Afrikaner South African Recipes. Please read the information and follow all rules and guidelines to ensure the best possible outcome and the most delicious and long lasting snack

Biltong is a traditional South African dried meat snack that is typically made from beef, although it can also be made from game meats such as venison or ostrich. Beef is the most common and traditional meat used to make biltong, and it is often made with lean cuts such as silverside or topside. However, some people also use other cuts of beef such as sirloin or flank steak. Ultimately, the choice of meat for making biltong will depend on personal preference, as well as the availability of different types of meat. It's important to use fresh, high-quality meat and follow proper food safety guidelines when making biltong.

If you are making biltong for the first time, it's important to follow proper food safety guidelines to avoid the risk of food poisoning. Make sure to use fresh, high-quality meat, clean and sanitize all utensils and surfaces, and keep the meat at a safe temperature while it is marinating and drying. Biltong can last for several weeks or even months if it is kept in an airtight container in a cool, dry place. However, the exact length of time that biltong will last depends on a few factors, such as the humidity and temperature of the storage environment, the type of meat used, and how the biltong was prepared.

Generally, the drier the biltong, the longer it will last. If the biltong is not completely dried, it may spoil more quickly. Additionally, if the biltong was not properly marinated or if it was made with low-quality meat, it may spoil more quickly as well.

To ensure that your biltong lasts as long as possible, it's important to store it in an airtight container in a cool, dry place. You can also store biltong in the refrigerator or freezer to extend its shelf life even further. Just be sure to allow the biltong to come to room temperature before eating it, as cold biltong can be tough and chewy.

Wet and Fatty Biltong

Some people may prefer their biltong to be wetter or fattier, which can be achieved through different preparation techniques.

Here are a few tips:

Wet biltong: If you prefer your biltong to be wetter and more tender, you can marinate the meat for a shorter amount of time or use a marinade with a higher moisture content. You can also add a small amount of liquid (such as beer or apple cider) to the marinade to help keep the meat moist. Just be careful not to add too much liquid, as this can cause the meat to spoil more quickly.

Fatty biltong: Biltong is traditionally made with lean cuts of meat, but you can add some fat to the meat before drying it if you prefer a fattier biltong. One way to do this is to use a fattier cut of meat, such as brisket or ribeye. You can also add a small amount of fat (such as bacon fat) to the marinade or rub the meat with oil or butter before drying it. Just be aware that adding fat to the meat can increase the risk of spoilage, so make sure to store the biltong properly and consume it within a reasonable amount of time.

Keep in mind that these techniques can alter the flavor and texture of the biltong, so it's important to experiment and find what works best for your taste preferences. Additionally, it's important to follow proper food safety guidelines when making biltong, as improper preparation or storage can lead to foodborne illness.

The key to making great biltong is to use high-quality meat, to marinate it well, and to ensure that it dries properly. Experiment with different spices and marinades to find the perfect recipe for your taste buds.

Some tips for marinating meat for biltong:

• Use a non-reactive container, such as a glass or ceramic bowl, to avoid any metallic or acidic flavors from the marinade.

• Make sure that the meat is completely coated in the marinade to ensure that the flavors are evenly distributed.

• You can adjust the amount of salt and spices to your taste preferences.

• Some people like to add a bit of brown sugar to the marinade to add a touch of sweetness to the biltong.

• You can experiment with different types of vinegar, such as apple cider vinegar or malt vinegar, to add a unique flavor to your biltong.

• If you're using a tougher cut of meat, you can add a bit of pineapple juice to the marinade to help tenderize the meat.

• Remember that the quality of the meat and the marinade will have a big impact on the final product, so use high-quality ingredients and take the time to marinate the meat properly for the best results.

BILTONG VARIATIONS

There are several variations of biltong, which differ based on the type of meat used, the seasoning and spices, and the method of preparation. Some of the most common types of biltong include:

• Beef biltong: The most popular type of biltong, made from beef cuts such as silverside, topside, or sirloin.

• Game biltong: Made from game meats such as kudu, springbok, or ostrich, which have a more intense flavor.

• Chicken biltong: A leaner, healthier option made from chicken breast, which is marinated and spiced before being dried.

• Fish biltong: Made from fish fillets that are marinated and dried, which results in a chewy, jerky-like texture.

• Bacon biltong: Made from bacon strips that are marinated and dried, which results in a crispy, crunchy texture.

Beef biltong *Ostrich biltong* *Chicken biltong* *Fish biltong* *Bacon biltong*

Biltong Recipes

Garlic Biltong

2-3 lbs beef *(silverside, topside, sirloin or flank steak)*
1/4 cup vinegar
1/4 cup Worcestershire sauce
1/4 cup soy sauce
1/4 cup brown sugar
1 tsp salt
1 tsp ground black pepper
1 tsp paprika
1 tsp garlic powder
Biltong spice *(optional)*

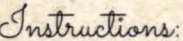

Instructions:

1. Trim any fat off the meat and cut it into thin strips, about 1/4 inch thick.
2. In a bowl, mix together the vinegar, Worcestershire sauce, soy sauce, brown sugar, salt, black pepper, paprika, and garlic powder. If you have biltong spice, you can add a tablespoon or two to the mixture as well.
3. Add the meat strips to the marinade, making sure that each strip is fully coated. Cover the bowl with plastic wrap and marinate the meat in the fridge for at least 4 hours or up to 24 hours.
4. After marinating, remove the meat strips from the marinade and pat them dry with a paper towel.
5. Hang the meat strips in a well-ventilated area to dry. You can use a biltong box, a dehydrator, or simply hang the meat on hooks in a dry, cool, and well-ventilated area. The drying process will take around 2-5 days, depending on the thickness of the meat and the humidity in your environment. Make sure to turn the meat strips every 12 hours or so to ensure even drying.
6. Once the meat is fully dried, slice it into thin pieces and enjoy!
7. Biltong should be kept in airtight container for longer shelf life.

Coriander Seed Biltong

Ingredients:

2-3 lbs beef *(silverside, topside, sirloin or flank steak)*
1/2 cup malt vinegar
1/4 cup Worcestershire sauce
1/4 cup soy sauce
1 tbsp coriander seeds, crushed
1 tbsp black pepper, freshly ground
1 tsp salt
1 tsp brown sugar
Biltong spice *(optional)*

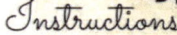

Instructions:

1. Trim any fat off the meat and cut it into thin strips, about 1/4 inch thick.
2. In a bowl, mix together the malt vinegar, Worcestershire sauce, soy sauce, coriander seeds, black pepper, salt, brown sugar, and biltong spice (if using).
3. Add the meat strips to the marinade, making sure that each strip is fully coated. Cover the bowl with plastic wrap and marinate the meat in the fridge for at least 6 hours or up to 24 hours.
4. After marinating, remove the meat strips from the marinade and pat them dry with a paper towel.
5. Hang the meat strips in a well-ventilated area to dry. You can use a biltong box, a dehydrator, or simply hang the meat on hooks in a dry, cool, and well-ventilated area. The drying process will take around 2-5 days, depending on the thickness of the meat and the humidity in your environment. Make sure to turn the meat strips every 12 hours or so to ensure even drying.
6. Once the meat is fully dried, slice it into thin pieces
7. Biltong should be kept in airtight container for longer shelf life.

Beer Biltong

Ingredients:

2-3 lbs beef *(silverside, topside, sirloin or flank steak)*
1 cup beer *(lager or ale)*
1/2 cup red wine vinegar
1/4 cup Worcestershire sauce
1/4 cup soy sauce
1 tbsp coriander seeds, crushed
1 tbsp black pepper, freshly ground
1 tsp salt
1 tsp brown sugar
Biltong spice *(optional)*

Instructions:

1. Trim any fat off the meat and cut it into thin strips, about 1/4 inch thick.
2. In a bowl, mix together the beer, red wine vinegar, Worcestershire sauce, soy sauce, coriander seeds, black pepper, salt, brown sugar, and biltong spice (if using).
3. Add the meat strips to the marinade, making sure that each strip is fully coated. Cover the bowl with plastic wrap and marinate the meat in the fridge for at least 6 hours or up to 24 hours.
4. After marinating, remove the meat strips from the marinade and pat them dry with a paper towel.
5. Hang the meat strips in a well-ventilated area to dry. You can use a biltong box, a dehydrator, or simply hang the meat on hooks in a dry, cool, and well-ventilated area. The drying process will take around 2-5 days, depending on the thickness of the meat and the humidity in your environment. Make sure to turn the meat strips every 12 hours or so to ensure even drying.
6. Once the meat is fully dried, slice it into thin pieces and enjoy!

The beer in this recipe adds a subtle flavor to the biltong and helps to tenderize the meat. If you prefer a stronger beer flavor, you can use a darker or more flavorful beer. Just be aware that using too much beer can make the biltong too wet and increase the risk of spoilage, so it's best to stick to the recommended amount.

"Taste the heritage of the Afrikaner people!"

Red Wine Vinegar Biltong

Ingredients:

2-3 lbs beef *(silverside, topside, sirloin or flank steak)*
1/2 cup red wine vinegar
1/4 cup Worcestershire sauce
1/4 cup soy sauce
2 tbsp coriander seeds, crushed
1 tbsp black pepper, freshly ground
1 tsp salt
Biltong spice *(optional)*

Instructions:

1. Trim any fat off the meat and cut it into thin strips, about 1/4 inch thick.
2. In a bowl, mix together the red wine vinegar, Worcestershire sauce, soy sauce, coriander seeds, black pepper, salt, biltong spice.
3. Add the meat strips to the marinade, making sure that each strip is fully coated. Cover the bowl with plastic wrap and marinate the meat in the fridge for at least 6 hours or up to 24 hours.
4. After marinating, remove the meat strips from the marinade and pat them dry with a paper towel.
5. Hang the meat strips in a well-ventilated area to dry. You can use a biltong box, a dehydrator, or simply hang the meat on hooks in a dry, cool, and well-ventilated area.
6. The drying process will take around 2-5 days, depending on the thickness of the meat and the humidity in your environment. Make sure to turn the meat strips every 12hrs or so to ensure even drying.
7. Once the meat is fully dried, slice into thin pieces & enjoy!

Garlic Bacon Biltong

Ingredients:

1 pound bacon
2 tablespoons kosher salt
1 tablespoon brown sugar
1 tablespoon coarsely ground black pepper
1 tablespoon paprika
1 tablespoon garlic powder
1 tablespoon onion powder
1/2 cup white vinegar

Instructions:

1. Cut the bacon into strips, about 1 inch wide.
2. In a bowl, mix together the kosher salt, brown sugar, black pepper, paprika, garlic powder, and onion powder.
3. Place the bacon strips in a large resealable plastic bag & sprinkle the spice mixture over the bacon, coating both sides evenly.
4. Pour the white vinegar over the bacon, distribute it evenly.
5. Seal the bag and refrigerate for at least 4 hours, or overnight.
6. Preheat your oven to 150°F (65°C).
7. Line a baking sheet with parchment paper.
8. Remove the bacon from the bag and pat dry with paper towels. Discard the excess liquid and spices.
9. Lay the bacon strips on the prepared baking sheet, making sure they do not touch each other.
10. Bake the bacon in the oven for 3-4hrs, until it is dry and crispy.
11. Let the bacon biltong cool before storing in an airtight container.

Basic Biltong

Ingredients:

2-3 lbs beef *(silverside, topside, sirloin or flank steak)*
1 cup vinegar
1 cup brown sugar
1 cup salt
1/4 cup coriander seeds, crushed
1 tbsp black pepper, freshly ground
1 tbsp bicarbonate of soda

Instructions:

1. Trim any fat off the meat and cut it into thin strips, +- 1/4 inch thick.
2. Mix together the vinegar, brown sugar, salt, coriander seeds, black pepper, bicarbonate of soda in a bowl to create a marinade.
3. Dip each meat strip into the marinade, making sure that each strip is fully coated. Place the strips in a non-reactive container, such as a glass or ceramic dish.
4. Pour the remaining marinade over the meat, making sure that it's fully covered.
5. Cover the container with plastic wrap and marinate the meat in the fridge for at least 6 hours or up to 24 hours.
6. After marinating, remove the meat strips from the marinade and pat them dry with a paper towel.
7. Hang the meat strips in a well-ventilated area to dry. You can use a biltong box, a dehydrator, or simply hang the meat on hooks in a dry, cool, and well-ventilated area. The drying process will take around 2-5 days, depending on the thickness of the meat and the humidity in your environment. Make sure to turn the meat strips every 12 hours or so to ensure even drying.
8. Once the meat is fully dried, slice it into thin pieces and enjoy!

This recipe uses a simple marinade of vinegar, sugar, and salt, with added coriander and black pepper for flavor. The bicarbonate of soda helps to tenderize the meat and also helps to preserve it. Remember to use high-quality meat and to dry the meat properly to get the best results.

Worcestershire Sauce Bacon Biltong

Ingredients:

1 pound of bacon
1/2 cup of kosher salt
1/2 cup of brown sugar
1 tablespoon of black pepper
1 tablespoon of paprika
1 tablespoon of garlic powder
1 tablespoon of onion powder
1 tablespoon of Worcestershire sauce

Instructions:

1. Mix together the kosher salt, brown sugar, black pepper, paprika, garlic powder, and onion powder in a small bowl.
2. Take the bacon and lay it flat in a shallow dish or container.
3. Pour the Worcestershire sauce over the bacon and rub it in well.
4. Sprinkle the spice mixture over the bacon, making sure to cover it evenly on both sides.
5. Cover the dish with a lid or plastic wrap and place it in the fridge for at least 24-48 hours, depending on how thick the bacon is and how dry you want it.
6. Check the bacon every 12 hours or so and pour off any accumulated liquid.
7. After the desired drying time, remove the bacon from the container and wipe off any excess spice mixture with a paper towel.
8. Slice into thin strips, and enjoy your homemade bacon biltong!

Basic Chicken Biltong

Ingredients:

2 lbs boneless, skinless chicken breasts
1/4 cup brown sugar
2 tablespoons coarse salt
2 teaspoons ground coriander
1 teaspoon garlic powder
1 teaspoon ground black pepper
1/2 teaspoon ground cloves
1/2 teaspoon cayenne pepper

Instructions:

1. Begin by cleaning and trimming the chicken breasts, removing any excess fat and sinew.
2. In a small bowl, mix together the brown sugar, coarse salt, coriander, garlic powder, black pepper, cloves, & cayenne pepper.
3. Rub the seasoning mixture over both sides of the chicken breasts, making sure to coat them evenly.
4. Place the chicken in a large ziplock bag or a covered container and refrigerate for at least 2 hours, but preferably overnight to allow the flavors to develop.
5. Preheat your biltong box or dehydrator to 140°F (60°C).
6. Remove the chicken from the refrigerator and pat it dry with paper towels.
7. Hang the chicken strips in the biltong box or dehydrator, making sure to leave space between them to allow for proper air circulation.
8. Dry the chicken for 3 to 5 hours, or until it reaches your desired texture. Check on it regularly and rotate the strips if necessary.
9. Once the chicken is done, remove it from the biltong box or dehydrator and let it cool completely before slicing it into thin strips.

"Kos maak die man!" -
"Food makes the man!"

(This phrase highlights the importance of good food in building strength and character.)

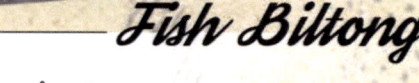

Garlic Chicken Biltong

Ingredients:

2 lbs boneless, skinless chicken breasts
1/4 cup kosher salt
1/4 cup brown sugar
2 tbsp coriander seeds
2 tbsp black pepper
1 tbsp paprika
1 tsp cumin
1 tsp garlic powder
1/2 tsp cayenne pepper

Instructions:

1. In a small pan over medium heat, toast the coriander seeds until fragrant, about 1-2 minutes. Let them cool, then grind them in a spice grinder or mortar and pestle.
2. In a small bowl, mix together the salt, brown sugar, coriander, black pepper, paprika, cumin, garlic powder, and cayenne pepper.
3. Cut the chicken into strips about 1 inch wide and 1/4 inch thick.
4. Coat the chicken strips with the spice mixture, making sure to cover them evenly.
5. Place the chicken strips in a single layer on a wire rack over a baking sheet. Leave some space between the strips so air can circulate around them.
6. Put the baking sheet in the refrigerator and let the chicken dry for at least 24-48 hours, until the strips are firm & dry to the touch.
7. Store the chicken biltong in an airtight container at room temperature for up to 2 weeks.

Fish Biltong

Ingredients:

1 pound of bacon
1/2 cup of kosher salt
1/2 cup of brown sugar
1 tablespoon of black pepper
1 tablespoon of paprika
1 tablespoon of garlic powder
1 tablespoon of onion powder
1 tablespoon of Worcestershire sauce

Instructions:

1. Mix together the kosher salt, brown sugar, black pepper, paprika, garlic powder, and onion powder in a small bowl.
2. Take the bacon and lay it flat in a shallow dish or container.
3. Pour the Worcestershire sauce over the bacon and rub it in well.
4. Sprinkle the spice mixture over the bacon, making sure to cover it evenly on both sides.
5. Cover the dish with a lid or plastic wrap and place it in the fridge for at least 24-48 hours, depending on how thick the bacon is and how dry you want it.
6. Check the bacon every 12 hours or so and pour off any accumulated liquid.
7. After the desired drying time, remove the bacon from the container and wipe off any excess spice mixture with a paper towel.
8. Slice into thin strips, and enjoy your homemade bacon biltong!

Notes

Notes

The Great Trek

Die Groot Trek or The Great Trek, as it was later called by South African historian George McCall Theal in the late 19th century, played a significant role in shaping the history and demographics of South Africa.

At the time of the Great Trek, which began in the 1830s, the Cape Colony had already been under British dominion since 1806. The British rule fostered resentment within the Boer community as they felt marginalized by the policies imposed on them. Fear of losing their Afrikaner culture, along with land disputes, political conflict and ongoing border wars with the Xhosas, forced the Boers to take action.

As a result, approximately 14 000 individuals, men, women and children, embarked on a historic journey into the interior regions of South Africa. They believed that by moving away from the British-controlled Cape Colony, they would find the much romanticised Promised Land that would provide them with the personal freedom, religious freedom, prosperity, and independence they desired. This group of people would later be referred to as the Voortrekkers (*Pioneers*).

However, they couldn't just pack up and move. The move necessitated careful planning and preparation.

Three exploration commissions were sent ahead of the Great Trek to survey the interior and identify potential settlement areas. One commission traveled to Natal, another explored as far as Soutpansberg, and a third journeyed through Bushmanland to an area in Damaraland. Little is known about the specific findings and feedback from these exploration commissions. However, it is likely that their observations and assessments played a significant role in the Voortrekkers' (*Pioneers*) decisions regarding the most desirable routes for their journey.

The Great Trek originated from the Eastern border districts of the Cape Colony, such as Graaff-Reinet, Uitenhage, Somerset-Oos, Tarka, Grahamstad, Cradock, and Colesberg. These districts served as the starting points for the Voortrekkers' (*Pioneers*) journey into the interior of South Africa.

To the North of the Cape Colony, the region was inhabited by various black tribes, among them the influential Zulus in present-day KwaZulu-Natal. The Zulu Kingdom, under the leadership of King Chaka, had emerged as a formidable power, having united several tribes into a powerful empire. The presence of powerful African kingdoms made the Voortrekkers' (*Pioneers*) journey into South Africa's interior that much more complex and challenging.

With ox-drawn wagons, pack animals, horses or even by foot, the Voortrekkers (*Pioneers*) embarked on a daring expedition into the unknown.

Several groups left the Cape Colony at various times during the Great Trek. Piet Retief led a group who left the Cape Colony in 1836. They traveled towards present-day KwaZulu-Natal. Andries Pretorius led a group who departed from the Cape Colony in 1838. They established the Republic of Natalia in present-day KwaZulu-Natal. Gerrit Maritz led a group who left the Cape Colony in 1838. They traveled northward towards present-day Pretoria in Gauteng. Sarel Cilliers led a group who left the Cape Colony in 1838. They settled in present-day Pietermaritzburg in KwaZulu-Natal. Hendrik Potgieter led a group who departed from the Cape Colony in 1839. They moved eastward towards present-day Mpumalanga and established settlements in that region.

The Voortrekkers (*Pioneers*) took great care in packing items vital for their survival, daily needs, and overall well-being. Among their belongings were provisions like preserved meat, grains, and non-perishable food items. They also carried cooking utensils, tools necessary for farming and construction, clothing, bedding, and weapons for protection. Additionally, they brought along livestock such as oxen and cattle, serving both as means of transportation and a sustainable food source. Remarkably, they also made room for personal possessions, sentimental items, and religious materials, emphasizing the importance of maintaining a sense of identity and spirituality throughout their challenging journey. Sadly, many family members could not join the Great Trek, being either too old or sickly to survive the journey. Promises of reunions were made and, ultimately, kept. Family reunification remained an important goal for many Voortrekkers (*Pioneers*) throughout the Great Trek.

The reality of The Great Trek was harsh and unforgiving. They faced so many hardships including disease, conflicts with indigenous populations and severe environmental conditions. Several hundred individuals, including men, women, and children, lost their lives during the Great Trek.

The Voortrekkers (*Pioneers*) played a significant role in shaping the early history and cultural identity of South Africa.

Ultimately, their actions paved the way for the eventual formation of the Boer republics and laid the foundation for the Afrikaner identity and cultural heritage.

A drawing of the Voortrekker monument, which was to be inaugurated in Pretoria in 1949, as it appeared eleven years earlier in an advertisement by the University of Pretoria, which introduced itself in it as the "Voortrekker University", and appeared in Die Huisgenoot's Commemorative Edition for the Great Trek, December 1938.

"The Great Trek remains a watershed moment in South African history, marking the beginning of the Voortrekkers' *(Pioneers)* quest for self-determination and shaping the future trajectory of the country." - *Hermann Giliomee*

"The Great Trek was a response to political and social conditions, leaving a lasting impact on the Afrikaner people and their collective identity." - *Albert Grundlingh*

How did the Great Trek influence the way traditional South Africans prepare and preserve food?

The Great Trek, or Die Groot Trek, as South Africans know it, was a major historical event in South Africa that took place between 1835 and 1854. It involved the migration of Dutch-speaking settlers, known as Boers, who left the British-controlled Cape Colony in search of freedom and new territories. The pioneers, or Voortrekkers, faced numerous challenges during the Great Trek, and their survival can be attributed to several factors:

Determination and Self-sufficiency:
The pioneers were driven by a strong desire for independence and religious freedom. They were self-reliant and resourceful, relying on their own skills and knowledge to survive. They were skilled farmers, hunters, and craftsmen who knew how to make use of the natural resources available to them.

Knowledge of the Land:
Many of the Boers had experience living in rural and frontier environments. They had knowledge of the local geography, climate, and natural resources, which helped them navigate and adapt to their new surroundings during the trek.

Ox-Wagon Transport:
The pioneers traveled in ox-drawn wagons, which provided them with mobile homes and a means to transport their belongings, supplies, and families. The wagons were sturdy and designed for long journeys, allowing them to traverse challenging terrains and carry essential provisions.

Hunting and Gathering:
Along the way, the pioneers relied on hunting and gathering to supplement their food supplies. They hunted game, fished in rivers and lakes, and gathered edible plants and fruits to sustain themselves during the journey.

Bartering and Trade:
The pioneers engaged in bartering and trade with indigenous communities they encountered. They exchanged goods such as livestock, tools, and clothing for food, water, and other necessities, establishing mutually beneficial relationships.

Formation of Communities:
The pioneers traveled in groups, forming communities and establishing campsites along their routes. This provided mutual support, security, and shared resources among the trekkers.

Adaptation and Resilience:
The pioneers faced various challenges, including harsh climates, diseases, hostile encounters with indigenous tribes, and limited access to resources. However, their adaptability, resilience, and determination to succeed helped them overcome these difficulties and continue their journey.

It is important to note that the Great Trek was not without conflict and hardships, and the pioneers faced significant struggles and losses along the way. However, their survival can be attributed to their resourcefulness, knowledge, and strong sense of purpose in seeking a better life in new territories.

Survival of The Fittest

Harde Koekies
(Hard Tack)

Ingredients:

4 cups (500g) all-purpose flour
1.5 cups (350ml) water
1 tsp (5g) salt

Instructions:

1. Preheat your oven to 375°F (190°C).
2. In a large mixing bowl, combine the flour and salt.
3. Gradually add in the water, stirring with a wooden spoon until a stiff dough forms.
4. Turn the dough out onto a lightly floured surface and knead it for about 10 minutes, until it becomes smooth and elastic.
5. Roll the dough out to a thickness of about 1/2 inch (1.25cm).
6. Cut the dough into squares or rectangles, about 3 inches (7.5cm) across.
7. Place the pieces of dough onto a baking sheet lined with parchment paper.
8. Bake the hard tack for about 30 minutes, or until it becomes dry and crisp.
9. Remove the hard tack from the oven and allow it to cool completely.
10. Store the hard tack in an airtight container at room temperature for up to several months.

Moderne Harde Koekies
(Modern Hard Tack)

Ingredients:

3 cups (360g) all-purpose flour
1 cup (240ml) water
1 tsp (5g) salt
1 tbsp (15g) honey *(optional)*

Instructions:

1. Preheat your oven to 250°F (120°C).
2. In a large mixing bowl, combine the flour, salt, and honey (if using). Mix well.
3. Gradually add the water to the flour mixture, stirring with a wooden spoon until a stiff dough forms.
4. Knead the dough on a lightly floured surface for a few minutes until it is smooth and elastic.
5. Roll out the dough into a thin sheet, about 1/4 inch (6mm) thick.
6. Use a sharp knife or pizza cutter to cut the dough into small, uniform pieces, about 3 inches (7.5cm) square.
7. Use a toothpick or skewer to poke several holes in each piece of dough.
8. Place the dough pieces on a baking sheet lined with parchment paper.
9. Bake the hardtack for 2-3 hours, or until they are completely dried out and hard.
10. Remove the hardtack from the oven and let them cool completely.
11. Store the hardtack in an airtight container or plastic bag until ready to use.

Note: You can adjust the flavor of the hardtack by adding different spices or herbs to the dough, such as cinnamon, garlic powder, or rosemary. You can also use whole grain flour or add other grains, such as oats or barley, to increase the nutritional value.

Roasted Corn

Parched corn is a simple and delicious snack made by roasting dried corn kernels until they are lightly toasted and crispy. Parched corn has a long history as a staple food among Native American tribes, who would roast corn in a fire or over hot coals.

Ingredients:

1 cup dried corn kernels
1-2 tablespoons vegetable oil
Salt, to taste

Instructions:

1. Heat a large skillet over medium-high heat.
2. Add the dried corn kernels to the skillet and shake the pan to spread the kernels into a single layer.
3. Toast the kernels for about 5-10 minutes, stirring occasionally, until they start to turn golden brown and become fragrant.
4. Remove the skillet from the heat and let the corn cool for a few minutes.
5. Once the corn has cooled, transfer it to a bowl and add the vegetable oil, tossing the kernels to coat them evenly.
6. Return the corn to the skillet and place it over medium-high heat.
7. Toast the kernels for another 5-10 minutes, stirring occasionally, until they are crispy and lightly browned.
8. Remove the skillet from the heat and sprinkle the parched corn with salt to taste.
9. Serve the parched corn as a snack or side dish.

Note: If you don't have dried corn kernels, you can use canned or frozen corn. Simply drain or thaw the corn and pat it dry with paper towels before toasting it in the skillet.

Loopgraafkoek Ingredients

Loopgraafkoek
(Trench Cake)

Loopgraafkoek is a type of cake that originated in Britain during World War I. It was created as a way to send cakes to soldiers on the front lines, as they could be transported and stored for long periods of time without spoiling. Loopgraafkoek is a simple but flavorful cake made with basic ingredients, and it has a rich history and tradition associated with it.

Ingredients:

1 cup (225g) self-raising flour
1/2 cup (115g) brown sugar
1/2 cup (115g) raisins or sultanas
1/2 cup (115g) currants
1/2 cup (115g) chopped walnuts or almonds
1/2 tsp ground cinnamon
1/2 tsp ground ginger
1/2 tsp ground nutmeg
1/2 cup (115g) margarine or butter
2 tablespoons (30ml) milk

Instructions:

1. Preheat your oven to 350°F (180°C).
2. In a large mixing bowl, combine the flour, sugar, raisins or sultanas, currants, chopped nuts, and spices.
3. Melt the margarine or butter in a small saucepan over low heat.
4. Add the milk to the melted margarine or butter and stir to combine.
5. Pour the melted margarine or butter mixture into the dry ingredients and stir until a stiff batter forms.
6. Grease a 9-inch (23cm) cake tin and line it with parchment paper.
7. Pour the batter into the prepared cake tin and smooth the surface with a spatula.
8. Bake the cake for 45-50 minutes, or until it is golden brown and a toothpick inserted into the center comes out clean.
9. Remove the cake from the oven and let it cool in the tin for 10min.
10. Remove the cake from the tin, cool completely on a wire rack.
11. Serve the trench cake as is, or sprinkle it with powdered sugar for a decorative touch.

Note: You can also add other dried fruits or spices to the trench cake, such as dates, figs, cloves, or allspice, to customize the flavor to your liking.

Vetkoek
(Fried Dough)

As the Boers settled in different parts of South Africa, they brought their tradition of making Vetkoek with them. The recipe evolved over time, and people added different ingredients like sugar, milk, and butter to the dough. Today, Vetkoek is a beloved snack that is enjoyed in South Africa.

Ingredients:

3 cups (375g) all-purpose flour
1 tbsp (15g) baking powder
1 tsp (5g) salt
1 cup (240ml) warm water
Oil for frying

Instructions:

1. In a large mixing bowl, combine the flour, baking powder, and salt. Mix well.
2. Gradually add the warm water to the flour mixture, stirring with a wooden spoon until a soft dough forms.
3. Knead the dough on a lightly floured surface for a few min. until it is smooth and elastic.
4. Cover the dough with a clean towel and let it rest for 10-15min.
5. Heat about 1 inch (2.5cm) of oil in a deep frying pan over medium-high heat.
6. Divide the dough into 8-10 equal pieces, roll each piece into a ball.
7. Flatten each ball of dough with your hands or a rolling pin into a thin, round disk, about 1/4 inch (6mm) thick.
8. Carefully place one or two pieces of dough in the hot oil and fry them for about 2-3min on each side, or until they are golden brown and crispy.

9. Use a slotted spoon or tongs to remove the fried bread from the oil and drain them on a paper towel-lined plate.
10. Repeat the process with the remaining pieces of dough, adding more oil to the pan as needed.
11. Serve the fry bread warm with your favorite toppings, such as ground beef, shredded cheese, lettuce, tomatoes, and salsa for tacos or honey, jam, or powdered sugar for a dessert.

Note: If you don't want to use oil for frying, you can also bake the fry bread in a preheated oven at 400°F (200°C) for about 10-15min, or until they are cooked through and lightly browned.

Gemaalde Mielies
(Roasted Maize)

Ingredients:

1 cup (170g) whole kernel corn
1 cinnamon stick
2 tbsp (30g) brown sugar
1 tbsp (7g) ground cinnamon
1/4 tsp (1g) salt

Instructions:

1. Preheat your oven to 350°F (180°C).
2. Spread the whole kernel corn in a single layer on a baking sheet.
3. Roast the corn in the preheated oven for about 20-25 minutes, or until the kernels are lightly browned and fragrant.
4. Remove the corn from the oven and let it cool for a few minutes.
5. In a blender or food processor, grind the roasted corn into a fine powder.
6. In a medium saucepan, bring 2 cups (480ml) of water and the cinnamon stick to a boil.
7. Add the ground corn, brown sugar, ground cinnamon, and salt to the boiling water.
8. Reduce the heat to low and stir the mixture continuously for about 10-15 minutes, or until it thickens to a porridge-like consistency.
9. Remove the cinnamon stick and let the pinole cool for a few minutes before serving.
10. Serve the pinole as a hot or cold beverage or use it as a base for other dishes.

Note: You can adjust the sweetness and spice level of the pinole by adding more or less sugar and cinnamon. You can also experiment with adding other spices or ingredients, such as vanilla extract or cocoa powder, to create different flavor profiles.

Flat Corn Bread

Ingredients:

1 cup (120g) yellow cornmeal
1/2 tsp (2g) salt
1 cup (240ml) boiling water
2 tbsp (28g) butter, softened
Oil for frying

Instructions:

1. In a medium mixing bowl, combine the cornmeal and salt. Mix well.
2. Gradually pour the boiling water into the cornmeal mixture, stirring with a wooden spoon until a thick dough forms.
3. Add the softened butter to the dough and mix well.
4. Cover the dough with a clean towel and let it rest for 10-15min.
5. Heat about 1/2 inch (1.25cm) of oil in a deep frying pan over medium-high heat.
6. Divide the dough into 8-10 equal pieces and roll each piece into a ball.
7. Flatten each ball of dough with your hands into a thick disk, about 2-3 inches (5-7.5cm) in diameter.
8. Carefully place one or two pieces of dough in the hot oil and fry them for about 2-3 minutes on each side, or until they are golden brown and crispy.
9. Use a slotted spoon or tongs to remove the fried corn dodgers from the oil and drain them on a paper towel-lined plate.
10. Repeat the process with the remaining pieces of dough, adding more oil to the pan as needed.
11. Serve warm with butter, syrup, or your favorite toppings.

Note: If you don't want to fry the corn dodgers, you can also bake them in a preheated oven at 375°F (190°C) for about 15-20min, or until they are cooked through and lightly browned.

Flat Corn Bread

Notes

Notes

President Paul Kruger

A Prominent Chapter in South African History

Stephanus Johannes Paulus Kruger, also known as Paul Kruger, was born on October 10, 1825, in the town of Bulhoek in the British Cape Colony.

As a child, Paul Kruger displayed remarkable resilience and determination, coming from a family with a strong history of resistance against colonial rule. Growing up among the Boer settlers, he developed a deep sense of independence and love for his people, shaping his future path.

In his youth, Paul Kruger embarked on a journey of self-discovery, mastering skills such as horse riding and marksmanship, which proved valuable later in life. Travelling through the vast landscapes of South Africa, he witnessed firsthand the injustices suffered by his people under British rule.

In 1852, Paul Kruger played a pivotal role in the signing of the Sand River Convention, which acknowledged the independence of the Transvaal region. This marked the beginning of his political career, and he gained respect within the Boer community.

During the First Boer War in 1880, Paul Kruger emerged as a prominent leader, rallying his people to defend their independence. Despite being outnumbered and outgunned, the Boers fought with unwavering determination, leading to the recognition of Transvaal's independence by the British.

Paul Kruger's leadership during the war garnered widespread admiration, and in 1883, he was elected as the President of the South African Republic, serving four consecutive terms. Under his guidance, Transvaal experienced progress in education, infrastructure, and the economy.

Kruger House

However, conflict resurfaced in the form of the Second Boer War in 1899, as the British sought dominance over the region. Despite his advancing age, President Paul Kruger stood firm, leading his people through the trials of war.

Ultimately, the British Empire prevailed, and in 1900, Paul Kruger was compelled to seek refuge in Europe, living the rest of his life in exile yearning for his beloved South Africa's freedom and independence.

On July 14, 1904, in leaving behind a to his people's rights continued shaping Clarens, Switzerland, Paul Kruger passed away, legacy of resilience and unwavering commitment and freedom. Despite dying in exile, his spirit to inspire generations, playing a crucial role in South Africa's future.

President Paul Kruger's life exemplified the indomitable spirit of the South African people, their struggle for independence, and their unwavering pursuit of freedom.

His story serves as a reminder of the sacrifices made by those who fought for the nation's liberation and their unyielding dedication to justice and equality.

Statue of Paul Kruger in Kruger National Park

The statue of Paul Kruger on Church Square in central Pretoria

1897 Two Shilling

General Koos de la Ray

The Lion of the Western Transvaal: A Tale of Bravery and Military Genius in the South African War

General Koos de la Rey, born Jacobus Herculaas de la Rey on October 22, 1847, was a prominent Boer military leader during the late 19th and early 20th centuries in South Africa. He played a significant role in the Boer Wars, which were fought between the British Empire and the Boers, primarily of Dutch descent, who inhabited the regions of Transvaal and Orange Free State.

De la Rey grew up in a farming community in the Marico district of the South African Republic (Transvaal). He gained a reputation as a skilled marksman and a tough and resourceful farmer. His involvement in military affairs began during the First Boer War (1880-1881), where he fought against British forces as a field cornet, a local officer rank.

However, it was during the Second Boer War (1899-1902) that De la Rey emerged as one of the most respected Boer commanders. He quickly rose through the ranks and became a general, leading successful military campaigns against the British forces. De la Rey's military strategy focused on mobile warfare and guerrilla tactics, utilizing the knowledge of the terrain and the ability to strike swiftly before disappearing into the vast South African landscape.

One of De la Rey's notable contributions to the Boer cause was his role in the Battle of Magersfontein in December 1899. As the British forces advanced towards Kimberley, De la Rey, along with other Boer commanders, devised a plan to halt their progress. They selected a defensive position at Magersfontein, taking advantage of the natural landscape, which included a series of ridges and trenches. De la Rey commanded the Boer forces on the western flank and successfully repelled several British attacks, causing heavy casualties among their ranks. The battle ended in a Boer victory, highlighting De la Rey's tactical brilliance.

Another significant battle in which De la Rey played a prominent role was the Battle of Modder River in November 1899. The British forces, under the command of General Methuen, attempted to cross the Modder River in order to relieve the besieged town of Kimberley. However, De la Rey's troops fiercely defended their positions, inflicting heavy casualties on the British forces and effectively halting their advance. Although the battle ended inconclusively, the Boers managed to maintain control of the region.

De la Rey continued to lead his forces in various engagements throughout the war, becoming a symbol of Boer resistance. His charisma and reputation as a skilled commander attracted many Boers to join the fight against the British. However, the war eventually took its toll on the Boer forces, and they were forced to surrender in May 1902.

Following the war, De la Rey pursued a political career, advocating for the rights of the Boer people. He opposed British policies and worked towards reconciliation between the Boers and the British. During World War I, he initially supported the German cause but later distanced himself from the conflict, promoting unity among South Africans.

Tragically, on September 15, 1914, De la Rey was killed in a case of mistaken identity during a confrontation with the police. His death shocked and deeply saddened both Boers and British alike, leading to an outpouring of grief and memorial services across the country.

General Koos de la Rey remains an important figure in South African history, revered for his military leadership and his efforts to unite the people of South Africa. His legacy serves as a reminder of the courage and determination displayed by the Boer fighters during their struggle for independence.

Jacobus Herculaas de la Rey (22 Oct. 1847 – 15 Sept. 1914), better known as Koos de la Rey, was a South African military officer who served as a Boer general during the Second Boer War.

De la Rey also had a political career and was one of the leading advocates of Boer independence.

Interesting Fact:

Bok van Blerk, a South African musician, wrote the song "De La Rey" as a tribute to General Koos de la Rey. The song was released in 2006 and became highly popular in South Africa, sparking national debate and resonating with a sense of Afrikaner identity and heritage.

Memorial at Magersfontein to fallen Scandinavian soldiers from the Battle of Magersfontein

Magersfontein Battlefield
(Kimberley, South Africa)

Battle of Tweebosch

DE KUNDE ICKE VIKA
11·DEC·1899
BLOTT FALLA KUNDE DE
TILL MINNE AV HÄR STUPADE SKANDINAVER

Potbrood

(Pot Bread)

A Bun in the (Dutch) Oven

A Dutch oven is a type of heavy cooking pot that is typically made of cast iron or enameled cast iron. It has a tight-fitting lid and thick walls that help to distribute heat evenly, making it ideal for slow-cooking and braising. The Dutch oven is believed to have originated in the Netherlands in the 17th century, where it was used for cooking soups, stews, and other hearty dishes. Dutch settlers later brought the pot to the United States, where it became a popular cooking vessel in frontier and pioneer cooking.

Today, Dutch ovens are still used for a variety of cooking tasks, both indoors and outdoors. They are often used for making stews, soups, and chili, as well as for baking bread and roasting meats. The heavy construction of the pot allows it to retain heat for a long time, which makes it ideal for slow-cooking dishes that require low and steady heat. Dutch ovens come in various sizes and shapes, and can be used on a variety of cooking surfaces, including stovetops, ovens, and campfires. They are often considered a versatile and durable cooking tool that can last for many years if properly cared for.

What is Potbrood?

Potbrood is a type of bread that is traditionally baked in a pot over an open fire or in a Dutch oven. It is a popular type of bread in South Africa and is also known as "potbread" or "potjiekos bread." The recipe for potbrood typically includes flour, yeast, salt, and water. The dough is mixed together and then placed in a pot or Dutch oven that has been heated over a fire or stove. The pot is then covered with a lid and the bread is left to bake for several hours, until it is golden brown and cooked through.

Potbrood has a dense, chewy texture and a slightly smoky flavor from being baked over an open fire. It is often served alongside stews, soups, and other hearty dishes and is especially popular during outdoor gatherings and camping trips.

Did you know you can even bake bread under the sand? Cooking bread under the sand is a traditional method of baking bread in many cultures around the world, and it can be a fun and unique way to prepare bread while camping or spending time outdoors. Here's a basic method for cooking bread under the sand:

1. Start by preparing your bread dough. You can use any bread recipe you like, but keep in mind that you'll need to adjust the cooking time and temperature for the sand oven. Make sure the dough is well-kneaded and has risen properly.

2. Choose a spot on the beach or in your backyard where the sand is clean and dry. Dig a hole in the sand that is large enough to fit your bread pan or Dutch oven. The hole should be deep enough to cover the bread completely with sand.

3. Build a fire nearby and let it burn down to coals. You'll need enough coals to fill the hole you've dug in the sand.

4. Place your bread pan or Dutch oven in the hole, making sure it is level and stable. Carefully pour the coals around the pan, making sure they are evenly distributed.

5. Cover the pan completely with sand, making sure there are no air pockets. The sand should be at least 2-3 inches thick on all sides.

6. Let the bread bake in the sand for about 1-2 hours, depending on the size of the bread and the heat of the coals. Check the bread periodically by carefully removing the sand and uncovering the pan. The bread is done when it is golden brown and sounds hollow when tapped on the bottom.

7. Use a shovel or tongs to carefully remove the bread from the sand. Brush off any excess sand and let the bread cool for a few minutes before slicing and serving.

Note that cooking bread under the sand can be a bit unpredictable, so be prepared to adjust the cooking time and temperature based on the heat of your coals and the size of your bread. It may take some trial and error to get it right, but the end result is a delicious, rustic bread with a unique flavor and texture.

(Pot Bread)
Potbrood Recipes

Raisin Potbrood

Ingredients:

4 cups bread flour (480g)
1 1/2 tsp. salt (7.5g)
2 tsp. active dry yeast (7g)
2 cups warm water (473ml)
1 tbsp. honey (21g)
1/4 cup melted butter or oil (60ml or 57g)
1/4 cup raisins (optional) (40g)

Instructions:

1. In a large mixing bowl, combine the bread flour, salt, and active dry yeast. If using raisins, add them to the dry ingredients.
2. In a separate bowl, mix together the warm water, honey, and melted butter or oil.
3. Add the wet ingredients to the dry ingredients and mix until a dough forms. Knead the dough on a floured surface for 5-10min, or until it is smooth and elastic.
4. Place the dough in a greased Dutch oven or cast iron pot. Cover the pot with a lid and let the dough rise for 1-2 hours, or until it has doubled in size.
5. Preheat your oven to 350 degrees Fahrenheit.
6. Bake the potbrood in the Dutch oven or pot for 50-60 minutes, or until the bread is golden brown and cooked through.
7. Carefully remove the potbrood from the Dutch oven or pot and let it cool on a wire rack before slicing and serving.
8. Optional: You can sprinkle the top of the bread with additional raisins or oats before baking for added texture and flavor. Serve the potbrood warm with butter, jam, or honey. Enjoy!

Potbrood

Ingredients:

3 cups (360g) bread flour
1 1/2 tsp. (8g) salt
1 tsp. (3g) active dry yeast
1 1/4 cups (296ml) warm water
1 tbsp. (21g) honey or sugar
1 tbsp. (14ml) vegetable oil or melted butter

Instructions:

1. In a large mixing bowl, combine the bread flour, salt, and active dry yeast.
2. In a separate bowl, mix together the warm water, honey or sugar, and vegetable oil or melted butter.
3. Add the wet ingredients to the dry ingredients and mix until a dough forms. Knead the dough on a floured surface for 5-10 minutes, or until it is smooth and elastic.
4. Place the dough in a greased Dutch oven or cast iron pot. Cover the pot with a lid and let the dough rise for 1-2 hours, or until it has doubled in size.
5. Preheat your oven to 350 degrees Fahrenheit.
6. Bake the potbrood in the Dutch oven or pot for 30-40 minutes, or until the bread is golden brown and cooked through.
7. Carefully remove the potbrood from the Dutch oven or pot and let it cool on a wire rack before slicing and serving.
8. Optional: You can add in additional ingredients such as herbs, cheese, or nuts to customize the flavor of your potbrood. Simply mix them into the dough before letting it rise.

Honey Potbrood

Ingredients:

- 4 cups bread flour (500g)
- 2 tsp. salt (10g)
- 2 tsp. active dry yeast (7g)
- 1 1/2 cups warm water (355 ml)
- 2 tbsp. honey (30 ml)
- 1/4 cup chopped fresh herbs (15g) *(rosemary / thyme or parsley)*
- 1/4 cup grated Parmesan cheese (optional) (25g)

Instructions:

1. In a large mixing bowl, combine the bread flour, salt, and active dry yeast. If using Parmesan cheese, add it to the dry ingredients.
2. In a separate bowl, mix together the warm water and honey.
3. Add the wet ingredients to the dry ingredients and mix until a dough forms. Knead the dough on a floured surface for 5-10 minutes, or until it is smooth and elastic.
4. Mix in the chopped fresh herbs to the dough.
5. Place the dough in a greased Dutch oven or cast iron pot. Cover the pot with a lid and let the dough rise for 1-2 hours, or until it has doubled in size.
6. Preheat your oven to 350 degrees Fahrenheit.
7. Bake the potbrood in the Dutch oven or pot for 40-50 minutes, or until the bread is golden brown and cooked through.
8. Carefully remove the potbrood from the Dutch oven or pot and let it cool on a wire rack before slicing and serving.
9. Optional: You can sprinkle the top of the bread with additional herbs and Parmesan cheese before baking for added flavor. Serve the potbrood warm with olive oil or balsamic vinegar for dipping. Enjoy!

"Honey is the taste of Freedom"

(This quote is often attributed to the Voortrekker (Pioneers) leader Piet Retief, who was known for his love of honey.)

Basil Potbrood

Ingredients:

- 4 cups bread flour (480 grams)
- 1 tsp. salt (6 grams)
- 2 tsp. active dry yeast (7 grams)
- 1 1/2 cups warm water (355 milliliters)
- 1/4 cup olive oil (60 milliliters)
- 1/4 cup chopped sun-dried tomatoes (40 grams)
- 2 tbsp. chopped fresh basil (6 grams)

Instructions:

1. In a large mixing bowl, combine the bread flour, salt, and active dry yeast. If using sun-dried tomatoes and fresh basil, add them to the dry ingredients.
2. In a separate bowl, mix together the warm water and olive oil.
3. Add the wet ingredients to the dry ingredients and mix until a dough forms. Knead the dough on a floured surface for 5-10min, or until it is smooth and elastic.
4. Mix in the chopped sun-dried tomatoes & fresh basil to the dough.
5. Place the dough in a greased Dutch oven or cast iron pot. Cover the pot with a lid and let the dough rise for 1-2 hours, or until it has doubled in size.
6. Preheat your oven to 350 degrees Fahrenheit.
7. Bake the potbrood in the Dutch oven or pot for 40-50 minutes, or until the bread is golden brown and cooked through.
8. Carefully remove the potbrood from the Dutch oven or pot and let it cool on a wire rack before slicing and serving.
9. Optional: You can sprinkle the top of the bread with additional fresh basil before baking for added flavor. Serve the potbrood warm with a drizzle of olive oil or balsamic vinegar. Enjoy!

Chopped Nuts Potbrood

Ingredients:

- 3 cups (360g) bread flour
- 1 tsp. salt (5g)
- 1 tsp. active dry yeast (3g)
- 1 1/4 cups (300ml) warm water
- 1 tbsp. (15ml) honey or sugar
- 1/4 cup (30g) chopped nuts *(such as walnuts or pecans)*
- 1/4 cup (30g) dried fruit *(such as cranberries or apricots)*

Instructions:

1. In a large mixing bowl, combine the bread flour, salt, and active dry yeast. If using nuts and dried fruit, add them to the dry ingredients.
2. In a separate bowl, mix together the warm water & honey/sugar.
3. Add the wet ingredients to the dry ingredients & mix until a dough forms. Knead the dough on a floured surface for 5-10 minutes, or until it is smooth and elastic.
4. Mix in the chopped nuts and dried fruit to the dough.
5. Place the dough in a greased Dutch oven or cast iron pot. Cover the pot with a lid and let the dough rise for 1-2 hours, or until it has doubled in size.
6. Preheat your oven to 350 degrees Fahrenheit.
7. Bake the potbrood in the Dutch oven or pot for 40-50 minutes, or until the bread is golden brown and cooked through.
8. Carefully remove the potbrood from the Dutch oven or pot and let it cool on a wire rack before slicing and serving.
9. Optional: You can sprinkle the top of the bread with additional nuts and dried fruit before baking for added texture and flavor. Serve the potbrood warm with butter or cream cheese for a delicious breakfast or snack. Enjoy!

Pot Bread

Notes

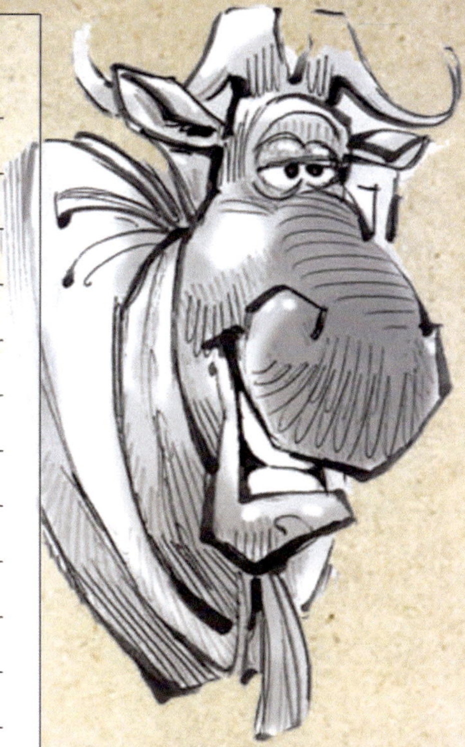

_____

_____

_____

_____

_____

_____

_____

_____

_____

_____

_____

_____

_____

_____

_____

_____

_____

Notes

_____

_____

_____

_____

_____

_____

_____

_____

_____

_____

_____

_____

_____

_____

_____

_____

_____

Racheltjie de Beer

A moving story of hardship, sacrifice and selfless love set against the harsh backdrop of the South African bushveld during the Great Trek.

As you journey along the N3 towards Kwa-Zulu Natal, near Van Reenens Village, take a moment to explore the charming Historic Church and the age-old Green Lantern wayside inn. It is in this very area that the captivating story of Racheltjie de Beer unfolded.

Just north of the village lies De Beer's Pass, an ancient road that stretches from Gauteng (Transvaal) to Natal. Named after Herman de Beer, a farmer who lived atop the majestic Drakensberg in the late 1870s, the pass holds a tale of fierce snowstorms and icy winds that ravage the region during winter. These natural elements pose a great threat to the animals, as temperatures plummet rapidly, often leading to fatal consequences if they are not provided with swift shelter.

One winter, Herman de Beer welcomed a fellow traveler with the same last name, De Beer, accompanied by his wife and their two children—a six-year-old boy and a twelve-year-old girl. Seeking to purchase a farm in the area, they arrived with a modest herd of cattle, sheep, and goats. The biting cold of the season added an extra layer of difficulty to their circumstances.

With a kind heart, Herman offered them refuge in the Hartebeest-house on his farm until they could secure a suitable plot of land. Little did they know that a tempestuous storm was looming on the horizon, dark clouds gathering and an icy wind cutting through the air. No amount of clothing could shield them from the bitter cold that permeated their surroundings.

Everyone on the farm rallied together to gather the cattle, ensuring their safety. The young animals from the previous lambing season were carefully transported to the warmth of the barn, while the remaining herd was herded into the kraal. De Beer, the prospective farm owner, had a small number of cattle and could ill afford to lose any. As he took inventory of his animals, he noticed that a calf was missing. Given their proximity to the hartebeest-house, it seemed plausible to track the calf's trail.

With daylight fading quickly, Racheltjie, who often assisted her father with the cattle, was asked to search for the calf closest to the house. Her father and his helper ventured further into the distance. Racheltjie's younger brother insisted on joining her, and with their mother's consent, they set off, ensuring they remained within close reach of the house. Wrapping her brother in a protective sheepskin, Racheltjie cautioned against straying too far.

Determined to locate their father's lost cattle before the impending snowstorm, Racheltjie and her little brother trudged through the winter landscape. Despite being warned about the approaching storm, their resolve remained unyielding. However, fate had a different plan in store for them. Disoriented within the blinding snow, they lost their way back home.

As the night grew darker, the temperature dropped, and Rachel realized the imminent danger her young brother faced—freezing to death in the frigid wilderness. Desperate to protect him, she scoured the surroundings for shelter and stumbled upon an abandoned anthill. With unwavering determination, she dug out its interior, creating a small, warm sanctuary for her brother. Placing her own body at the entrance, she shielded him from the relentless wind and snow.

Aware that her own survival was unlikely, Rachel prayed for strength and courage. Throughout the long, bitter night, she remained vigilant, her senses sharp despite the numbing cold. Meanwhile, their father and his helpers returned home long after darkness had swallowed the land, but Rachel and her brother were still missing. The snowstorm raged on, its fury turning snowflakes into ice, making it difficult to maintain direction, let alone see.

To guide the lost children back to safety, their mother ignited a roaring fire near the house, providing a beacon amidst the relentless storm. Bundled in blankets to shield themselves from the ferocity of the tempest, their father and two more helpers set off, lanterns in hand, determined to find their beloved children.

With the break of dawn, searchers stumbled upon Rachel's lifeless body outside the anthill, her final act of shielding the entrance serving as a testament to her unwavering love and sacrifice. Miraculously, her brother survived, cradled in the warmth of Rachel's affection and devotion.

The tale of Rachel de Beer's bravery and selflessness has become a treasured part of South African legend. Her memory remains cherished, symbolizing the indomitable spirit, courage, and resilience of the Voortrekkers. Her name echoes through time, a testament to the enduring power of sacrificial love amidst the harshest of trials.

Beer Bread Recipes

As the sun sets over the sweeping plains of the Highveld, the scent of freshly baked bread wafts through the air, drawing a group of Voortrekkers together. They gather around the kitchen table, their faces illuminated by the gentle flickering of a kerosene lamp. At the center of the table sits a golden loaf of beer bread, emanating warmth and enticing aromas.

This cherished recipe has been handed down through generations of Voortrekkers, a tradition that reaches back to the days of the Great Trek and remains alive in the present. It is a testament to their resourcefulness, ingeniously transforming humble ingredients such as flour, salt, and beer into a hearty, satisfying bread.

The beer used in the recipe is often a homemade brew, crafted from maize or barley. Its rich, earthy flavours infuse each bite with a distinctly South African taste. Beyond its culinary appeal, it symbolizes the resilience and ingenuity of the Voortrekker Boere, who made the most of what they had, turning simplicity into something exceptional.

As the group breaks off pieces of the warm bread and spreads them generously with farm butter, they delve into tales of their ancestors who ventured across the land, forging a new home. They recount the hardships they endured and the triumphs they achieved, all while relishing the simple pleasure of a freshly baked loaf.

For the Voortrekkers, these beer bread recipes hold a significance that extends beyond sustenance. They serve as a tangible link to their history and a joyous celebration of their culture. It is a reminder that even in the face of adversity, there are reasons to be grateful, and the act of breaking bread together binds them in unity and gratitude.

As the night deepens, their voices blend with laughter and camaraderie, echoing the spirit of their forefathers. The aroma of beer bread lingers in the air, carrying with it the stories of the past and the unwavering spirit of the Voortrekkers, a people who found solace, strength, and a sense of home in a simple loaf of bread.

Garlic & Herb Beer Bread

Ingredients:

3 cups (375 g) all-purpose flour
3 tsp (15 g) baking powder
1 tsp (5 g) salt
1/4 cup (50 g) granulated sugar
1 bottle (12 oz or 355 ml) beer
2 cloves garlic, minced
1 tbsp (1 g) fresh thyme, chopped
1 tbsp (1 g) fresh rosemary, chopped
1/4 cup (60 g) unsalted butter, melted

Instructions:

1. Preheat the oven to 375°F (190°C) and grease a 9x5-inch (23x13 cm) loaf pan.
2. In a large bowl, whisk together the flour, baking powder, salt, and sugar.
3. Add the minced garlic, chopped thyme, and chopped rosemary to the dry ingredients and stir until just combined.
4. Add the beer to the dry ingredients and stir until just combined.
5. Pour the mixture into the greased loaf pan.
6. Drizzle the melted butter over the top of the batter.
7. Bake for 45-50 minutes, or until a toothpick inserted into the center comes out clean.
8. Allow the bread to cool in the pan for 5-10 minutes before transferring it to a wire rack to cool completely.

Classic Beer Bread

Ingredients:

3 cups (375 g) all-purpose flour
3 tsp (15 g) baking powder
1 tsp (5 g) salt
1/4 cup (60 g) granulated sugar
12 oz (355 ml) beer, at room temperature
1/4 cup (56 g) unsalted butter, melted

Instructions:

1. Preheat the oven to 375°F (190°C).
2. In a large mixing bowl, whisk together the flour, baking powder, salt, and sugar.
3. Pour in the beer and stir until a sticky dough forms.
4. Transfer the dough to a greased loaf pan.
5. Pour the melted butter over the top of the dough.
6. Bake for 45-50 minutes or until a toothpick inserted into the center comes out clean.

Cheesy Beer Bread

Ingredients:

2 cups (250 g) all-purpose flour
1 tbsp (15 g) baking powder
1 tsp (5 g) salt
1/4 tsp (1 g) cayenne pepper
2 cups (200 g) shredded cheddar cheese
12 oz (355 ml) beer, at room temperature

Instructions:

1. Preheat the oven to 375°F (190°C).
2. In a large mixing bowl, whisk together the flour, baking powder, salt, and cayenne pepper.
3. Stir in the shredded cheddar cheese.
4. Pour in the beer and stir until a sticky dough forms.
5. Transfer the dough to a greased loaf pan.
6. Bake for 45-50 minutes or until a toothpick inserted into the center comes out clean.

Cheesy Jalapeno Beer Bread

Ingredients:

3 cups (375 g) all-purpose flour
3 tsp (15 g) baking powder
1 tsp (5 g) salt
1/4 cup (50 g) granulated sugar
1 bottle (12 oz or 355 ml) beer
1/2 cup (50 g) shredded cheddar cheese
2 jalapenos, seeded and diced
1/4 cup (60 g) unsalted butter, melted

Instructions:

1. Preheat the oven to 375°F (190°C) and grease a 9x5-inch (23x13 cm) loaf pan.
2. In a large bowl, whisk together the flour, baking powder, salt, and sugar.
3. Add the shredded cheddar cheese and diced jalapenos to the dry ingredients and stir until just combined.
4. Add the beer to the dry ingredients and stir until just combined.
5. Pour the mixture into the greased loaf pan.
6. Drizzle the melted butter over the top of the batter.
7. Bake for 45-50 minutes, or until a toothpick inserted into the center comes out clean.
8. Allow the bread to cool in the pan for 5-10 minutes before transferring it to a wire rack to cool completely.

Honey Wheat Beer Bread

Ingredients:

2 cups (250 g) whole wheat flour
1 cup (125 g) all-purpose flour
3 tsp (15 g) baking powder
1 tsp (5 g) salt
1/4 cup (60 ml) honey
1 bottle (12 oz or 355 ml) wheat beer
1/4 cup (60 g) unsalted butter, melted

Instructions:

1. Preheat the oven to 375°F (190°C) and grease a 9x5-inch (23x13 cm) loaf pan.
2. In a large bowl, whisk together the whole wheat flour, all-purpose flour, baking powder, and salt.
3. Add the honey and beer to the dry ingredients and stir until just combined.
4. Pour the mixture into the greased loaf pan.
5. Drizzle the melted butter over the top of the batter.
6. Bake for 45-50 minutes, or until a toothpick inserted into the center comes out clean.
7. Allow the bread to cool in the pan for 5-10 minutes before transferring it to a wire rack to cool completely.

Chocolate Stout Beer Bread

Ingredients:

2 cups (250 g) all-purpose flour
3/4 cup (60 g) unsweetened cocoa powder
1/2 cup (100 g) granulated sugar
1 tbsp (15 g) baking powder
1 tsp (5 g) salt
1 bottle (12 oz or 355 ml) chocolate stout beer
1/4 cup (60 ml) vegetable oil
1 egg
1/2 cup (90 g) semi-sweet chocolate chips

Instructions:

1. Preheat the oven to 350°F (180°C) and grease a 9x5-inch (23x13 cm) loaf pan.
2. In a large bowl, whisk together the flour, cocoa powder, sugar, baking powder, and salt.
3. In a separate bowl, whisk together the beer, vegetable oil, and egg.
4. Pour the wet ingredients into the dry ingredients and stir until just combined.
5. Fold in the chocolate chips.
6. Pour the batter into the greased loaf pan.
7. Bake for 45-50 minutes, or until a toothpick inserted into the center comes out clean.
8. Allow the bread to cool in the pan for 5-10 minutes before transferring it to a wire rack to cool completely.

A group of Afrikaans women at the centenary celebrations in 1938 dressed in Voortrekker (Pioneers) garb, most notably the white kappies or sunbonnets on their heads.

Cinnamon Raisin Beer Bread

Ingredients:

3 cups (375 g) all-purpose flour
3 tsp (15 g) baking powder
1 tsp (5 g) salt
1/4 cup (50 g) granulated sugar
1 bottle (12 oz or 355 ml) beer
1/2 cup (80 g) raisins
2 tsp (4 g) ground cinnamon
1/4 cup (60 g) unsalted butter, melted

Instructions:

1. Preheat the oven to 375°F (190°C) and grease a 9x5-inch (23x13 cm) loaf pan.
2. In a large bowl, whisk together the flour, baking powder, salt, and sugar.
3. Add the raisins and cinnamon to the dry ingredients and stir until just combined.
4. Add the beer to the dry ingredients and stir until just combined.
5. Pour the mixture into the greased loaf pan.
6. Drizzle the melted butter over the top of the batter.
7. Bake for 45-50 minutes, or until a toothpick inserted into the center comes out clean.
8. Allow the bread to cool in the pan for 5-10 minutes before transferring it to a wire rack to cool completely.

Chocolate Chip Beer Bread

Ingredients:

3 cups (375 g) all-purpose flour
3 tsp (15 g) baking powder
1 tsp (5 g) salt
1/2 cup (100 g) granulated sugar
1 bottle (12 oz or 355 ml) beer
1 cup (170 g) semisweet chocolate chips
1/4 cup (60 g) unsalted butter, melted

Instructions:

1. Preheat the oven to 375°F (190°C) and grease a 9x5-inch (23x13 cm) loaf pan.
2. In a large bowl, whisk together the flour, baking powder, salt, and sugar.
3. Add the chocolate chips to the dry ingredients and stir until just combined.
4. Add the beer to the dry ingredients and stir until just combined.
5. Pour the mixture into the greased loaf pan.
6. Drizzle the melted butter over the top of the batter.
7. Bake for 45-50 minutes, or until a toothpick inserted into the center comes out clean.
8. Allow the bread to cool in the pan for 5-10 minutes before transferring it to a wire rack to cool completely.

Rosemary & Olive Oil Beer Bread

Ingredients:

3 cups (375 g) all-purpose flour
3 tsp (15 g) baking powder
1 tsp (5 g) salt
1/4 cup (60 ml) olive oil
1 bottle (12 oz or 355 ml) beer
2 tbsp (4 g) fresh rosemary, finely chopped
1/4 cup (60 g) unsalted butter, melted

Instructions:

1. Preheat the oven to 375°F (190°C) and grease a 9x5-inch (23x13 cm) loaf pan.
2. In a large bowl, whisk together the flour, baking powder, and salt.
3. Add the olive oil and beer to the dry ingredients and stir until just combined.
4. Add the chopped rosemary to the batter and stir until evenly distributed.
5. Pour the mixture into the greased loaf pan.
6. Drizzle the melted butter over the top of the batter.
7. Bake for 45-50 minutes, or until a toothpick inserted into the center comes out clean.
8. Allow the bread to cool in the pan for 5-10 minutes before transferring it to a wire rack to cool completely.

Jalapeno Chedder Beer Bread

Ingredients:

3 cups (375 g) all-purpose flour
1 tbsp (15 g) baking powder
1 tsp (5 g) salt
1/2 cup (115 g) unsalted butter, melted
1 bottle (12 oz or 355 ml) beer
1 cup (115 g) shredded cheddar cheese
2 jalapeño peppers, seeded and finely chopped

Instructions:

1. Preheat the oven to 375°F (190°C) and grease a 9x5-inch (23x13 cm) loaf pan.
2. In a large bowl, whisk together the flour, baking powder, and salt.
3. Add the melted butter to the dry ingredients and stir until just combined.
4. Add the beer to the mixture and stir until just combined.
5. Fold in the shredded cheddar cheese and chopped jalapeño peppers.
6. Pour the batter into the greased loaf pan.
7. Bake for 45-50 minutes, or until a toothpick inserted into the center comes out clean.
8. Allow the bread to cool in the pan for 5-10 minutes before transferring it to a wire rack to cool completely.

Notes

_____
_____
_____
_____
_____
_____
_____
_____
_____
_____
_____
_____
_____
_____
_____

Notes

_____
_____
_____
_____
_____
_____
_____
_____
_____
_____
_____
_____
_____
_____
_____
_____
_____

Celebrating the Richness of Afrikaans

The Life and Legacy of C. Louis Leipoldt

C. Louis Leipoldt was an influential South African writer, poet, and physician who played a vital role in the development of Afrikaans language and culture. Born in 1880 in Worcester, a small town in South Africa's Western Cape province, Leipoldt grew up in a family that cherished literature and culture. He pursued medical studies in South Africa and England and practiced as a physician for many years. However, his passion for literature and writing remained unwavering, and he continued to create throughout his life.

In 1911, Leipoldt published his first collection of poems, titled "Gedigte" (Poems), which garnered praise from both critics and readers. Throughout his writing career, he delved into themes of nature, culture, and identity, with a particular focus on the Boer people and their struggles to preserve their cultural identity amidst British colonialism. His writing often exalted the natural beauty of South Africa and celebrated the distinctiveness of the Afrikaans language.

Leipoldt's work played a significant role in the advancement of Afrikaans language and culture, which had long been regarded as inferior to English. He firmly believed in the richness and expressiveness of Afrikaans and dedicated himself to promoting its usage in literature and everyday life.

In addition to his poetry and prose, Leipoldt wrote cookbooks and was known for his love of food and wine. He saw food as an integral part of culture and identity, advocating for the celebration and preservation of traditional Afrikaans dishes.

Beyond his literary and culinary pursuits, Leipoldt actively engaged in politics and was a prominent member of the Afrikaner nationalist movement. He advocated for the establishment of an independent state for the Boer people and fought for their rights throughout his lifetime.

Leipoldt passed away in 1947, but his legacy as a writer, physician, and champion of Afrikaans culture endures. He is widely recognized as one of the most significant figures in South African literature, revered for his contributions to Afrikaans language and culture. His work continues to inspire new generations of writers and thinkers who are dedicated to celebrating and preserving the diverse and vibrant cultural heritage of South Africa.

Various South African artists have transformed a well-known Leipoldt poem into a song. These words resonate with South African culture and reflect on love, longing, and memories:

C Louis Leipoldt (1880 – 1947)
Wys My Die Plek

Wys my die plek waar ons saam gestaan het,
Eens, toe jy myne was –
Vroeër, voor jou liefde vir my getaan het,
Vroeër, toe jy myne was.
Kyk, dis dieselfde; die silwer see
Blink in die sonskyn, soos lang verlee
Dit eenmaal geblink het, 'n welkomsgroet
Vir ons liefde wat uithou en alles vergoed.

Wys my die plek waar ons saam gekniel het,
Eens, toe jy myne was –
Vroeër, toe een siel vir ons saam besiel het,
Vroeër, toe jy myne was.
Kyk, dis dieselfde; die hemel, blou,
Lag soos voorheen op my en op jou;
Dit skitter nog altyd 'n welkomsgroet
Vir ons liefde wat uithou en alles vergoed.

Wys my die plek waar ons saam geloop het,
Eens, toe jy myne was –
Vroeër, toe ons harte so veel gehoop het,
Vroeër, toe jy myne was.
Kyk, dis dieselfde! Net jy nie. Vra,
Wie van ons twee moet die meeste dra?
Jy wat vergeet het – of ek wat boet
Vir my liefde wat uithou en alles vergoed?

English Translation:
Show Me the Place

Show me the place where we once stood together,
Once, when you were mine –
Earlier, before your love for me faded,
Earlier, when you were mine.
Look, it's the same; the silver sea
Shines in the sunshine, like long ago
It once gleamed, a welcome greeting
For our enduring love that compensates for everything.

Show me the place where we knelt together,
Once, when you were mine –
Earlier, when one soul inspired us both,
Earlier, when you were mine.
Look, it's the same; the sky, blue,
Laughs upon me and upon you like before;
It still sparkles, a welcome greeting
For our enduring love that compensates for everything.

Show me the place where we walked together,
Once, when you were mine –
Earlier, when our hearts held so much hope,
Earlier, when you were mine.
Look, it's the same! Only you aren't. Ask,
Who between us should bear the most?
You, who have forgotten – or me, who pays the price
For my love that endures and compensates for everything?

Christian Frederik Louis Leipoldt (28 Dec. 1880 – 12 Apr. 1947), usually referred to as C. Louis Leipoldt, was a South African poet, dramatist, medical doctor, reporter and food expert.

Rusk Recipes
Rusks of the Ages

South African rusks are a traditional type of baked good that originated in South Africa. They are a type of dry, crunchy biscuit that is usually eaten dipped in coffee or tea.

The history of South African rusks dates back to the Dutch settlers who arrived in South Africa in the 17th century. These settlers brought with them a traditional Dutch recipe for a type of bread that was baked twice to make it dry and crispy. This type of bread was known as "beschuit" in Dutch.

Over time, South African cooks began to adapt the recipe for beschuit to suit their own tastes and ingredients. They started adding more sugar, butter, and eggs to the recipe, which gave the rusks a richer flavor and texture. They also began to experiment with different flavors, such as adding buttermilk or raisins to the dough. South African rusks became especially popular in the 19th century, when they were a staple food for travelers and farmers who needed a sturdy, portable snack that could withstand long journeys and harsh weather conditions.

In fact, rusks were often referred to as "boerbeskuit," which means "farmer's biscuits" in Afrikaans. Today, South African rusks are still a popular snack and are available in a variety of flavors, such as buttermilk, muesli, and even chocolate chip. They are often enjoyed as a breakfast or tea-time snack, and are especially popular during the colder months of the year when people crave something warm and comforting to dunk in their hot beverages.

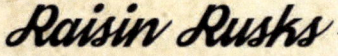

Vanilla Dream Rusks

Ingredients:

4 cups (500g) all-purpose flour
1 cup (200g) sugar
1 tsp salt
1 tbsp baking powder
2 eggs
1 cup (240ml) buttermilk
1 cup (240ml) vegetable oil
2 tsp vanilla extract
1 cup (150g) raisins *(optional)*

Instructions:

1. Preheat your oven to 350°F (180°C).
2. In a large mixing bowl, combine the flour, sugar, salt, and baking powder. Mix well.
3. In another bowl, whisk together the eggs, buttermilk, vegetable oil, and vanilla extract.
4. Add the wet ingredients to the dry ingredients and mix until you have a soft dough.
5. If you're using raisins, fold them into the dough.
6. Grease a 9x13 inch (23x33cm) baking dish and transfer the dough to the dish, spreading it out evenly.
7. Bake for 45-50 minutes or until the top is golden brown and a toothpick inserted in the center comes out clean.
8. Allow the rusks to cool completely in the dish, then remove them from the dish and cut them into rectangular pieces.
9. Reduce the oven temperature to 200°F (90°C) and arrange the rusks on a baking sheet.
10. Bake the rusks for 3-4 hours or until they are completely dry and hard. Turn them over every hour, ensure that they dry out evenly.
11. Once the rusks are completely dry, store them in an airtight container at room temperature.

Enjoy your homemade rusks as a delicious and crunchy snack with your tea or coffee!

Raisin Rusks

Ingredients:

3 cups (375g) all-purpose flour
1 cup (125g) whole wheat flour
1 cup (200g) sugar
1 tsp salt
1 tbsp baking powder
2 eggs
1 cup (240ml) milk
1/2 cup (120ml) vegetable oil
2 tsp vanilla extract
1 cup (150g) raisins *(optional)*

Instructions:

1. Preheat your oven to 350°F (180°C).
2. In a large mixing bowl, combine the all-purpose flour, whole wheat flour, sugar, salt, and baking powder. Mix well.
3. In another bowl, whisk together the eggs, milk, vegetable oil, and vanilla extract.
4. Add the wet ingredients to the dry ingredients and mix until you have a soft dough.
5. If you're using raisins, fold them into the dough.
6. Grease a 9x13 inch (23x33cm) baking dish and transfer the dough to the dish, spreading it out evenly.
7. Bake for 45-50 minutes or until the top is golden brown and a toothpick inserted in the center comes out clean.
8. Allow the rusks to cool completely in the dish, then remove them from the dish and cut them into rectangular pieces.
9. Reduce the oven temperature to 200°F (90°C) and arrange the rusks on a baking sheet.
10. Bake the rusks for 3-4 hours or until they are completely dry and hard. Turn them over every hour to ensure that they dry out evenly.
11. Once the rusks are completely dry, store them in an airtight container at room temperature.

Classic Buttermilk Rusks

Buttermilk Rusks

Ingredients:

4 cups (500g) whole wheat flour
2 cups (250g) all-purpose flour
1 cup (200g) sugar
1 tsp salt
1 tbsp baking powder
2 eggs
1 cup (240ml) buttermilk
1/2 cup (120ml) vegetable oil
2 tsp vanilla extract

Instructions:

1. Preheat your oven to 350°F (180°C).
2. In a large mixing bowl, combine the whole wheat flour, all-purpose flour, sugar, salt, and baking powder. Mix well.
3. In another bowl, whisk together the eggs, buttermilk, vegetable oil, and vanilla extract.
4. Add the wet ingredients to the dry ingredients and mix until you have a soft dough.
5. Grease a 9x13 inch (23x33cm) baking dish and transfer the dough to the dish, spreading it out evenly.
6. Bake for 45-50 minutes or until the top is golden brown and a toothpick inserted in the center comes out clean.
7. Allow the rusks to cool completely in the dish, then remove them from the dish and cut them into rectangular pieces.
8. Reduce the oven temperature to 200°F (90°C) and arrange the rusks on a baking sheet.
9. Bake the rusks for 3-4 hours or until they are completely dry and hard. Turn them over every hour to ensure that they dry out evenly.
10. Once the rusks are completely dry, store them in an airtight container at room temperature.

Raisin & Vanilla Rusks

Ingredients:

4 cups (500g) all-purpose flour
1 cup (200g) sugar
1 tsp salt
1 tbsp baking powder
2 eggs
1 cup (240ml) milk
1/2 cup (120ml) vegetable oil
2 tsp vanilla extract
1/2 cup (80g) raisins (optional)

Instructions:

1. Preheat your oven to 350°F (180°C).
2. In a large mixing bowl, combine the all-purpose flour, sugar, salt, and baking powder. Mix well.
3. In another bowl, whisk together the eggs, milk, vegetable oil, and vanilla extract.
4. Add the wet ingredients to the dry ingredients and mix until you have a soft dough.
5. If you're using raisins, fold them into the dough.
6. Grease a 9x13 inch (23x33cm) baking dish and transfer the dough to the dish, spreading it out evenly.
7. Bake for 45-50 minutes or until the top is golden brown and a toothpick inserted in the center comes out clean.
8. Allow the rusks to cool completely in the dish, then remove them from the dish and cut them into rectangular pieces.
9. Reduce the oven temperature to 200°F (90°C) and arrange the rusks on a baking sheet.
10. Bake the rusks for 3-4 hours or until they are completely dry and hard. Turn them over every hour to ensure that they dry out evenly.
11. Once the rusks are completely dry, store them in an airtight container at room temperature.

Almond Rusks

Ingredients:

4 cups (500g) all-purpose flour
1 cup (200g) sugar
1 tsp salt
1 tbsp baking powder
2 eggs
1 cup (240ml) milk
1/2 cup (120ml) vegetable oil
2 tsp vanilla extract
1 cup (150g) chopped almonds (optional)

Instructions:

1. Preheat your oven to 350°F (180°C).
2. In a large mixing bowl, combine the all-purpose flour, sugar, salt, and baking powder. Mix well.
3. In another bowl, whisk together the eggs, milk, vegetable oil, and vanilla extract.
4. Add the wet ingredients to the dry ingredients and mix until you have a soft dough.
5. If you're using almonds, fold them into the dough.
6. Grease a 9x13 inch (23x33cm) baking dish and transfer the dough to the dish, spreading it out evenly.
7. Bake for 45-50 minutes or until the top is golden brown and a toothpick inserted in the center comes out clean.
8. Allow the rusks to cool completely in the dish, then remove them from the dish and cut them into rectangular pieces.
9. Reduce the oven temperature to 200°F (90°C) and arrange the rusks on a baking sheet.
10. Bake the rusks for 3-4 hours or until they are completely dry and hard. Turn them over every hour, ensure that they dry out evenly.
11. Once the rusks are completely dry, store them in an airtight container at room temperature.

Yoghurt Rusks

Ingredients:

4 cups (500g) self-raising flour
1 tsp (5g) salt
1 cup (250g) sugar
4 cups (400g) oats
2 cups (500g) plain yogurt
1 cup (250g) vegetable oil
2 large eggs
1 tsp (5g) vanilla essence

Instructions:

1. Preheat your oven to 350°F (175°C).
2. In a large mixing bowl, sift together the self-raising flour and salt.
3. Add the sugar and oats to the mixing bowl and mix well.
4. In a separate mixing bowl, whisk together the plain yogurt, vegetable oil, eggs, and vanilla essence.
5. Add the wet ingredients to the dry ingredients and mix until everything is well combined.
6. Spread the mixture out onto a greased baking tray and bake in the preheated oven for 35-40 minutes, or until golden brown.
7. Remove the tray from the oven and let it cool for a few minutes before cutting the rusks into small squares or rectangles.
8. Reduce the oven temperature to 200°F (95°C).
9. Place the rusks back onto the baking tray and put them into the oven to dry out for about 3-4 hours, or until they are completely dry and crispy.
10. Store the rusks in an airtight container and enjoy as a tasty breakfast or snack!

Note: These measurements make a large batch of rusks, so feel free to halve the recipe if you prefer a smaller batch. Also, you can customize the recipe by adding in your favorite nuts, seeds, or dried fruit.

Rusks with Oats & Raisins

Multi Seed Rusks

Ingredients:

2 cups (250g) self-raising flour
1 tsp (5g) salt
1/2 cup (100g) sugar
1 cup (100g) oats
1/2 cup (50g) sunflower seeds
1/2 cup (50g) pumpkin seeds
1/4 cup (25g) sesame seeds
1/4 cup (25g) flaxseeds
1/4 cup (50ml) vegetable oil
1 cup (250ml) plain yogurt
2 large eggs

Instructions:

1. Preheat your oven to 350°F (175°C).
2. In a large mixing bowl, sift together the self-raising flour and salt.
3. Add the sugar, oats, sunflower seeds, pumpkin seeds, sesame seeds, and flaxseeds to the mixing bowl and mix well.
4. In a separate mixing bowl, whisk together the vegetable oil, plain yogurt, and eggs.
5. Add the wet ingredients to the dry ingredients and mix until everything is well combined.
6. Spread the mixture out onto a greased baking tray and bake in the preheated oven for 35-40 minutes, or until golden brown.
7. Remove the tray from the oven and let it cool for a few minutes before cutting the rusks into small squares or rectangles.
8. Reduce the oven temperature to 200°F (95°C).
9. Place the rusks back onto the baking tray and put them into the oven to dry out for about 3-4 hours, or until they are completely dry and crispy.
10. Store the seed rusks in an airtight container and enjoy as a tasty breakfast or snack!

Buttermilk & Seed Rusks

Ingredients:

2 cups (250g) whole wheat flour
1 tsp (5g) salt
1/4 cup (50g) honey
1/4 cup (50g) molasses
1/4 cup (50g) vegetable oil
1/2 cup (50g) sunflower seeds
1/2 cup (50g) pumpkin seeds
1/4 cup (25g) sesame seeds
1/4 cup (25g) flaxseeds
1 cup (250ml) buttermilk
2 large eggs

Note: If you don't have buttermilk on hand, you can substitute it with regular milk mixed with 1 tablespoon of lemon juice or vinegar.

Instructions:

1. Preheat your oven to 350°F (175°C).
2. In a large mixing bowl, sift together the whole wheat flour and salt.
3. Add the honey, molasses, vegetable oil, sunflower seeds, pumpkin seeds, sesame seeds, and flaxseeds to the mixing bowl and mix well.
4. In a separate mixing bowl, whisk together the buttermilk and eggs.
5. Add the wet ingredients to the dry ingredients and mix until everything is well combined.
6. Spread the mixture out onto a greased baking tray and bake in the preheated oven for 35-40 minutes, or until golden brown.
7. Remove the tray from the oven and let it cool for a few minutes before cutting the rusks into small squares or rectangles.
8. Reduce the oven temperature to 200°F (95°C).
9. Place the rusks back onto the baking tray and put them into the oven to dry out for about 3-4 hours, or until they are completely dry and crispy.
10. Store the seed rusks in an airtight container and enjoy as a tasty breakfast or snack!

Oats & Seeds Rusks

Ingredients:

2 cups (250g) self-raising flour
1 tsp (5g) salt
1/2 cup (100g) sugar
1 cup (100g) oats
1/2 cup (50g) sunflower seeds
1/2 cup (50g) pumpkin seeds
1/4 cup (25g) sesame seeds
1/4 cup (25g) flaxseeds
1/4 cup (50ml) vegetable oil
1 cup (250ml) plain yogurt
2 large eggs

Note: You can also customize this recipe by using different seeds or adding in your favorite nuts or dried fruit.

Instructions:

1. Preheat your oven to 350°F (175°C).
2. In a large mixing bowl, sift together the self-raising flour and salt.
3. Add the sugar, oats, sunflower seeds, pumpkin seeds, sesame seeds, and flaxseeds to the mixing bowl and mix well.
4. In a separate mixing bowl, whisk together the vegetable oil, plain yogurt, and eggs.
5. Add the wet ingredients to the dry ingredients and mix until everything is well combined.
6. Spread the mixture out onto a greased baking tray and bake in the preheated oven for 35-40 minutes, or until golden brown.
7. Remove the tray from the oven and let it cool for a few minutes before cutting the rusks into small squares or rectangles.
8. Reduce the oven temperature to 200°F (95°C).
9. Place the rusks back onto the baking tray and put them into the oven to dry out for about 3-4 hours, or until they are completely dry and crispy.
10. Store the seed rusks in an airtight container and enjoy as a tasty breakfast or snack!

Butter Rusks

Ingredients:

4 cups (500g) self-raising flour
1 tsp (5g) salt
1/2 cup (100g) sugar
1/2 cup (125g) butter or margarine
2 large eggs
1 cup (250ml) milk

Instructions:

1. Preheat your oven to 350°F (175°C).
2. In a large mixing bowl, sift together the self-raising flour and salt.
3. Add the sugar and butter/margarine to the mixing bowl, and use your fingertips to rub the butter/margarine into the flour mixture until it resembles coarse breadcrumbs.
4. Beat the eggs and milk together in a separate mixing bowl.
5. Add the wet ingredients to the dry ingredients and mix until everything is well combined and a soft dough forms.
6. Knead the dough on a lightly floured surface for a few minutes until it becomes smooth and elastic.
7. Roll the dough into a rectangular shape, +- 1 inch (2.5cm) thick.
8. Cut the dough into small squares or rectangles.
9. Place the rusks onto a greased baking tray and bake in the preheated oven for 25-30 minutes, or until golden brown.
10. Remove the tray from the oven & let it cool for a few min before separating the rusks & placing them back onto the baking tray.
11. Reduce the oven temperature to 200°F (95°C).
12. Put the rusks back into the oven to dry out for about 3-4 hours, or until they are completely dry and crispy.
13. Store the rusks in an airtight container and enjoy as a tasty breakfast or snack!

Notes

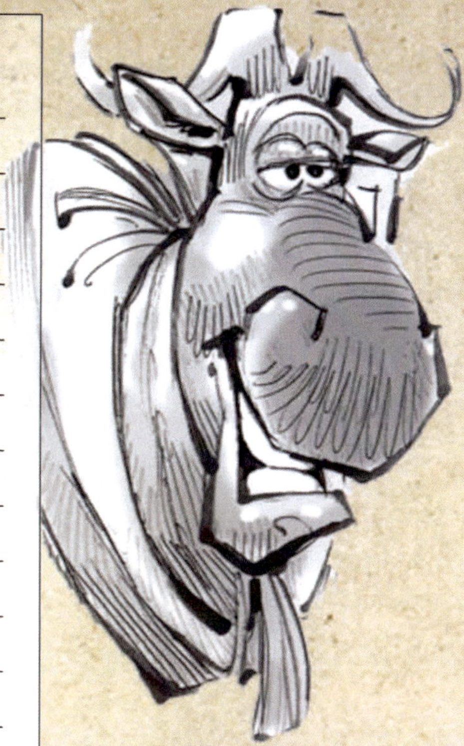

_____
_____
_____
_____
_____
_____
_____
_____
_____
_____
_____
_____
_____
_____
_____

Notes

_____
_____
_____
_____
_____
_____
_____
_____
_____
_____
_____
_____
_____
_____
_____
_____
_____
_____
_____

The Battle of Blood River

In the mid-1830s, a group of Voortrekkers (*Pioneers*), led by Andries Pretorius, departed from the Cape Colony and embarked on an inland journey in search of new lands for settlement. After enduring a long and arduous trek, they arrived at a valley nestled amidst the Drakensberg Mountains and along the banks of the Ncome River. This significant location would later be known as the site of the renowned Battle of Blood River.

The Voortrekkers (*Pioneers*), characterized by their independence, self-sufficiency, and determination, were Dutch-speaking settlers seeking a new home where they could freely practice their Christian faith without interference from the British colonial authorities, who held control over the Cape Colony at the time.

Upon reaching the valley, the Voortrekkers (*Pioneers*) encountered a formidable force of Zulu warriors led by the fearsome King Dingane. The Zulus had already defeated a previous group of Voortrekker (*Pioneers*) settlers led by Piet Retief, who had been negotiating with Dingane for land rights. Although Dingane had initially agreed to grant Retief's request in exchange for the return of stolen cattle, he treacherously ordered the execution of Retief and his men as soon as their end of the agreement was fulfilled.

Aware of the imminent danger, the Voortrekkers (*Pioneers*) prepared themselves for battle. They constructed trenches and formed a protective laager—a circular arrangement of wagons. Despite being significantly outnumbered, with approximately 464 men, women, and children, against an estimated 12,000 Zulu warriors, the Voortrekkers (*Pioneers*) remained resolute.

On the 16 December 1838 the Zulu Army numbering some 12 000 warriors and led by Ndlela kaNtuli attacked the Voortrekker Commando of some 464 armed men laagered on the banks of the Ncome River. The battle lasted most of the morning with the Zulus suffering heavy casualties before finally withdrawing.

Prior to the commencement of the battle on December 16, 1838, Pretorius gathered his men for prayer, seeking divine protection and guidance. He entered into a covenant with God, vowing that if they emerged victorious, they would construct a church in His honor. Additionally, the Voortrekkers (*Pioneers*) made a solemn promise to commemorate the battle annually on the same day, observing a day of fasting to express gratitude for God's safeguarding.

The clash began in the morning, with the Zulu army charging at the Voortrekker (*Pioneers*) laager. However, the Voortrekkers (*Pioneers*) were well-prepared and possessed superior firepower. Armed with muskets and rifles while the Zulus primarily wielded spears and shields, the Voortrekkers unleashed a devastating volley, inflicting heavy casualties upon the Zulu ranks. The battle persisted for several hours, marked by relentless Zulu charges repelled by the steadfast firepower of the Voortrekkers.

At the battle's conclusion, only three Voortrekkers (*Pioneers*) had perished, while several others sustained injuries. In contrast, the Zulu army suffered significant losses, with approximately 3,000 warriors killed and many more wounded. The Battle of Blood River proved to be a decisive triumph for the Voortrekkers (*Pioneers*), symbolizing their resilience and unwavering determination.

True to their pledge, the Voortrekkers (*Pioneers*) erected a church on the battlefield, later known as the Blood River Church. Today, this church stands as a testament to the bravery and faith of the Voortrekkers (*Pioneers*), attracting visitors who seek to delve into South Africa's rich history and culture. Annually, on December 16th, the Day of Reconciliation, the Battle of Blood River is commemorated as a significant event in the nation's history.

On the site are 64 full size replica bronze wagons set in the format of the original laager.

A Vow Sealed in Blood

Day of the Vow 16 December 1838

In the vast landscapes of South Africa, a determined group of Voortrekkers (Pioneers), under the leadership of Andries Pretorius, confronted a powerful Zulu force along the Ncome River. This significant battle took place on December 16, 1838, leaving an indelible mark on South African history.

The Rising Tensions

Tensions between the Voortrekkers, descendants of Dutch settlers, and the Zulu kingdom had escalated to a critical point. In their quest for freedom and independence, the Voortrekkers (*Pioneers*) ventured into uncharted territories, further intensifying the conflict.

The Day of Destiny

On this crucial day, they formed a laager, a circular defensive formation using ox-drawn wagons, in preparation of a battle that would significantly influence the fate of a nation for generations to follow.

The Battle of Blood River

Empowered by firearms and employing effective tactics, the Boers faced wave after wave of determined Zulu warriors intent on attacking and overcoming them. The battle unfolded with both sides fiercely engaged, marking a critical moment in South African history.

The Courageous Stand

After two hours and four waves of attack, with intermittent breaks allowing the Voortrekkers (*Pioneers*) to reload and rest, Pretorius instructed a group of horsemen to leave the camp and confront the Zulu, aiming to disrupt their formations. Although the Zulu resisted for a while, substantial losses forced them to disperse. The actual death toll was roughly estimated between 3,000 and 6,000 deceased Zulus, and three Pioneers suffered injuries. During the pursuit, Pretorius was wounded in his left hand by a Zulu spear. Among the 3,000-6,000 deceased Zulu soldiers, two were princes, making Ndlela's favorite, Prince Mpande, the leading contender in the subsequent battle for the Zulu crown.

A Price Paid and a Promise Honored

Four days after the Battle of Blood River, the Trekker (*Pioneer*) commando reached King Dingane's kraal, UmGungundlovu (located near present-day Eshowe). Upon arrival, they discovered the kraal had been abandoned and lay in ruins. Notably, the bones of Piet Retief, whom Dingane had previously murdered, along with those of his men, were located and respectfully buried. Today, a memorial stands at this site, commemorating the solemn events of that historical period.

The Legacy of the Day of the Vow

To this day, December 16th remains a public holiday in South Africa. Before 1994, it held various names such as "the Day of the Vow," "the Day of the Covenant," and "Dingaan's Day." However, it is now officially recognized as "the Day of Reconciliation."

A Call for Unity and Renewal

In today's world, where divisions seem to grow wider and conflicts more complex, it is time for a reawakening, a renewal, of that solemn vow made on the banks of the Ncome River. It is a call for Christians from all corners of the globe to come together, to stand united in faith, and to pray for healing, not just for a land in need but for a world in need.

A Timeless Lesson

For the lesson of the Vow Church and the Battle of Blood River is not confined to the pages of history. It is a timeless reminder that when people of faith unite and make a solemn vow to God, miracles can happen, and even the most daunting challenges can be overcome.

A Beacon of Hope

As we remember the Day of the Vow and the sacrifices made by those who came before us, let us also remember the vow they made—to never forget their faith, their unity, and the divine intervention that brought them victory. May we, as a global community of Christians, renew that vow and fervently pray for healing, peace, and unity in our troubled world.

In the Spirit of Unity

Draw inspiration from the unwavering faith demonstrated by the Voortrekkers (*Pioneers*). Find the strength to stand together, understanding that, in the words of Napoleon Bonaparte, 'The strong man is the one who can intercept at will the communication between the senses and the mind.' Let our shared faith act as the interceptors, breaking down the barriers that divide us and paving the way for a brighter, more united future.

Moordkoppie Monument Dingaanstat

A Call to Remember

And so, on this Day of the Vow, let us remember the lessons of history, the power of faith, and the strength of unity. May our vow to God be a beacon of hope and healing for our land and our world.

Bobotie Bounty

A Collection of Savory South African Delights

Bobotie is a dish that originated in South Africa and is considered a national dish. The name "bobotie" is derived from the Indonesian word "bobotok," which means "meatball." Bobotie is traditionally made with ground beef or lamb, but it can also be made with other meats such as chicken, pork, or ostrich.

The dish is flavored with a blend of spices such as curry powder, turmeric, cumin, and coriander, and is often sweetened with dried fruit such as raisins, apricots, or dates. Bobotie is typically served with a side of yellow rice, which is flavored with turmeric and raisins, and topped with a chutney made from fruit such as mango, apricot, or peach. In 1951, bobotie was declared a national dish of South Africa by the Cape Malay community.

Bobotie is not only a delicious dish, but it is also an important part of South African culture and history, representing the diverse culinary influences that have shaped the country's cuisine over the centuries.

Curried Beef with Almonds & Raisins

Ingredients:

1 kg (2.2 lbs) lean ground beef
2 onions, chopped
2 tbsp oil
2 tbsp butter
1 tbsp curry powder
1 tsp ground turmeric
2 tbsp sugar
1 tbsp apricot jam
2 tbsp chutney
3 tbsp vinegar
3 tbsp raisins
3 tbsp slivered almonds
4 slices of bread
2 cups (500 ml) milk
3 eggs
1 tsp salt
1/2 tsp black pepper

For the topping:
3 eggs
1 cup (250 ml) milk

Instructions:

1. Preheat the oven to 180°C (350°F).
2. Heat the oil and butter in a large pan and fry the onions until soft.
3. Add the curry powder and turmeric and fry for another minute.
4. Add the ground beef and fry until browned.
5. Add the sugar, apricot jam, chutney, vinegar, raisins, and almonds. Mix well and simmer for 10 minutes.
6. Soak the bread in the milk until soft, squeeze out the excess milk.
7. Add the bread to the meat mixture and mix well.
8. Beat the eggs and add them to the meat mixture, along with the salt and pepper. Mix well.
9. Spoon the mixture into a greased oven dish.
10. Beat the eggs for the topping and mix in the milk.
11. Pour the topping over the meat mixture.
12. Bake for 45 minutes, or until the topping is golden brown.

Spiced Beef with Bay Leaves

Ingredients:

1 kg (2.2 lb) ground beef
2 slices of bread
1 cup (240 ml) milk
2 tbsp vegetable oil
2 onions, chopped
1 tbsp curry powder
1 tbsp turmeric
2 tsp ground cumin
2 tsp ground coriander
1 tsp ground cinnamon
1 tsp ground ginger
3 tbsp apricot jam
2 tbsp white wine vinegar
1 tbsp Worcestershire sauce
1 tbsp sugar
1 tsp salt
1/2 tsp black pepper
3 eggs
10-12 bay leaves

For the topping:
1 cup (240 ml) milk
3 eggs
1/4 tsp salt

Instructions:

1. Preheat the oven to 350°F (180°C).
2. Soak the bread slices in 1 cup (240 ml) of milk for a few minutes.
3. Heat the vegetable oil in large pan, sauté the onions until softened.
4. Add the ground beef to the pan and cook until browned, breaking up any lumps with a wooden spoon.
5. Add the curry powder, turmeric, cumin, coriander, cinnamon, and ginger to the pan, and cook for a further 2-3 minutes.
6. Add the apricot jam, white wine vinegar, Worcestershire sauce, sugar, salt, and black pepper to the pan and mix well.
7. Squeeze the excess milk from the soaked bread slices, and add the bread to the pan. Mix well.
8. Beat 3 eggs and add them to the pan, mixing well.
9. Pour the mixture into a baking dish, press bay leaves into the top.
10. Bake in the preheated oven for 40-45min, until the top is golden brown and the filling is set.
11. To make the topping, whisk together 1 cup (240 ml) milk, 3 eggs, and 1/4 tsp salt.
12. Pour the topping over the cooked bobotie, and return to the oven for a further 10-15min, until the topping is set and golden brown.
13. Serve with yellow rice and chutney. Enjoy!

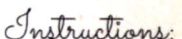
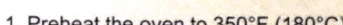

South African Bobotie

Mango & Coconut Chicken Curry Bobotie

Ingredients:

1 lb (450g) ground beef
2 slices of white bread, crusts removed, soaked in milk
1 large onion, chopped
2 cloves garlic, minced
1 tbsp (15 ml) vegetable oil
1 tbsp (15 ml) curry powder
1 tsp (5 ml) ground turmeric
1 tsp (5 ml) ground cumin
1 tsp (5 ml) ground coriander
1/2 tsp (2.5 ml) ground cinnamon
1/2 tsp (2.5 ml) ground ginger
1/2 cup (120 ml) beef stock
1 tbsp (15 ml) apricot jam
2 tbsp (30 ml) vinegar
1/2 cup (120 ml) raisins
3 eggs
Salt and pepper, to taste
Bay leaves, for garnish

For the topping:
1/2 cup (120 ml) milk
2 eggs

Instructions:

1. Preheat your oven to 350°F (180°C).
2. Heat the oil in a large skillet over medium heat. Add the onion and garlic and cook until softened, about 5 minutes.
3. Add the ground beef to the skillet and cook until browned and cooked through, about 10 minutes.
4. Add the curry powder, turmeric, cumin, coriander, cinnamon, and ginger to the skillet, stir to combine. Cook for 1-2min, until fragrant.
5. Add the beef stock, apricot jam, vinegar, and raisins to the skillet and stir to combine. Simmer for 10-15 minutes, until the sauce has thickened. Season with salt and pepper to taste.
6. Transfer the beef mixture to a large baking dish and smooth out the top with a spoon.
7. In a small bowl, whisk together the milk and eggs for the topping. Pour the mixture over the beef mixture in the baking dish.
8. Place a few bay leaves on top of the egg mixture.
9. Bake for 30-35 minutes, until the topping is golden brown and set.
10. Serve hot with rice and chutney.

Spicy Beef Bobotie

Ingredients:

1 kg (2.2 lbs) ground beef
2 slices white bread, crusts removed, soaked in water
2 onions, chopped
2 tbsp curry powder
2 tbsp apricot jam
2 tbsp vinegar
1 tbsp chutney
1 tbsp Worcestershire sauce
1 tbsp oil
1 tsp salt
1 tsp sugar
1/2 tsp turmeric
1/2 tsp black pepper
2 bay leaves
3 eggs
500 ml (2 cups) milk

For the topping:
4 eggs
125 ml (1/2 cup) milk
1/4 tsp salt
1/4 tsp turmeric
1/4 tsp black pepper

Instructions:

1. Preheat the oven to 180°C (350°F).
2. Heat the oil in a large pan and fry the onions until they are soft.
3. Add the curry powder, salt, sugar, turmeric & black pepper to the onions and fry for another minute.
4. Add the ground beef and fry until browned.
5. Add the apricot jam, vinegar, chutney & Worcestershire sauce to the pan and mix well.
6. Remove the bread from the water and squeeze out the excess water. Add the bread to the beef mixture and mix well.
7. Pour the beef mixture into an ovenproof dish and place the bay leaves on top.
8. Beat the eggs and milk together and pour over the beef mixture.
9. Bake for 30 minutes.
10. Beat the eggs, milk, salt, turmeric and black pepper together for the topping.
11. Remove the dish from the oven and pour the topping over the beef mixture.
12. Return the dish to the oven and bake for a further 20-30min, until the topping is set and golden brown.
13. Serve with yellow rice and *sambal.

South African Bobotie with Bay Leaves

Ingredients:

2 slices bread (50g / 1.8 oz)
250 ml (1 cup) milk
2 onions, chopped (200g / 7 oz)
2 tablespoons vegetable oil
1 kg (2.2 lbs) ground beef
2 tablespoons curry powder
1 tablespoon turmeric
1 tablespoon ground cumin
1 tablespoon ground coriander
2 cloves garlic, minced
2 tablespoons apricot jam
2 tablespoons chutney
1/2 cup (125 ml) almonds, chopped
1 tablespoon Worcestershire sauce

2 eggs, beaten
3 tablespoons vinegar
salt and pepper to taste
bay leaves for garnish

For the topping:
3 eggs
250 ml (1 cup) milk

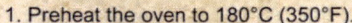

Instructions:

1. Preheat the oven to 180°C (350°F).
2. Soak the bread in the milk.
3. Fry the onions in the vegetable oil until soft.
4. Add the ground beef and brown.
5. Add the curry powder, turmeric, cumin, coriander, and garlic.
6. Cook for a few minutes until fragrant.
7. Add the apricot jam, chutney, vinegar, Worcestershire sauce, eggs, and almonds.
8. Mix well and season with salt and pepper.
9. Transfer the mixture to a greased oven dish & smooth the top.
10. Place the bay leaves on top.
11. Bake for 30 minutes.
12. Beat together the eggs and milk for the topping.
13. Pour over the bobotie and bake for an additional 15 minutes until set and golden brown.
14. Let the bobotie rest for a few minutes before serving.
15. Enjoy your delicious Bobotie!

Notes

Notes

The Battle of Majuba

It was the year 1881, and tensions between the British Empire and the Transvaal Republic, a Boer state in southern Africa, were running high. The British had been attempting to establish control over the region, but the fiercely independent Boers staunchly resisted British rule.

On February 27th, 1881, the two sides clashed in what would be remembered as the Battle of Majuba. Leading the British forces was Major General Sir George Pomeroy Colley, who ordered an advance up a steep hill to attack the Boer position. However, they encountered determined resistance from the Boers.

Under the leadership of Commandant General Piet Joubert, the Boers had strategically positioned themselves atop the hill, enjoying a clear advantage over the British troops below. Leveraging their superior marksmanship, they unleashed a relentless hail of gunfire, preventing the British from making any progress.

Despite suffering significant losses, Colley refused to retreat, firmly believing that his troops could prevail if they persisted. Nevertheless, the Boers held their ground, and as the day progressed, the morale of the British soldiers steadily declined.

In a final desperate attempt to alter the course of the battle, Colley ordered a charge up the hill. The Boers swiftly responded with a lethal onslaught of bullets, forcing the British into a hasty retreat within minutes.

The Battle of Majuba proved to be a devastating defeat for the British, resulting in over 200 casualties compared to the Boers' single casualty. The consequences of this defeat were far-reaching, effectively bringing an end to British efforts to assert control over the Transvaal Republic. It also marked a turning point in the conflict between the Boers and the British, instilling the Boers with newfound confidence and pride in their capabilities as soldiers.

Despite its significance, the Battle of Majuba has often been overshadowed and forgotten in historical accounts, eclipsed by other conflicts that occurred during the same period. However, for those who participated in the battle, it was a momentous event that profoundly shaped their lives and the destiny of their nations.

Commandant General P.J. Joubert Member of the Triumvirate In Office: (8 August 1881 - 9 May 1883), Serving with M.W. Pretorius and Paul Kruger

British officers observing Majuba Hill before the Battle of Majuba Hill on 27th February 1881 in the First Boer War.

(Dutch Oven)
Potjiekos Recipes

Potjiekos is a traditional South African dish that has its roots in the early history of the country. The word "potjiekos" literally means "small-pot food" in Afrikaans, which is one of the 11 official languages of South Africa.

The dish is believed to have originated with the Voortrekkers, who were a group of Dutch-speaking settlers who moved from the Cape Colony into the interior of South Africa during the 1830s. These settlers were largely nomadic and relied heavily on hunting for their food, which led to the development of the potjie as a cooking method.

The potjie is a cast-iron pot with three legs, designed to be placed directly on a fire. The pot is heated from the bottom and the food is cooked slowly over a low heat, which allows the flavors to meld together and creates a deliciously tender and flavorful dish.

Potjiekos is a communal dish, traditionally cooked and served in a social setting such as a family gathering, camping trip, or braai (barbecue). The dish is often made with meat, vegetables, and a variety of spices and herbs, depending on the recipe and the preferences of the cook.

Today, potjiekos remains a popular and beloved dish in South Africa, enjoyed by people of all backgrounds and cultures. It is often seen as a symbol of South African identity and a reminder of the country's rich history and diverse culinary traditions.

Traditional Potjiekos

Ingredients:

1.5 kg beef, cubed
2 onions, chopped
4 cloves garlic, minced
2-3 large carrots, sliced
2-3 potatoes *(peeled&cubed)*
2-3 sweet potatoes *(peeled&cubed)*
2-3 tomatoes, chopped
2-3 bay leaves
2-3 sprigs of thyme
2-3 sprigs of rosemary
1 cup beef stock
1 cup red wine
Salt and pepper
Olive oil

Instructions:

1. Heat some olive oil in your potjie pot over medium-high heat.
2. Add the beef cubes and brown them on all sides.
3. Remove the beef from the pot and set it aside.
4. Add a little more olive oil to the pot & then add the onions and garlic. Cook until the onions are translucent.
5. Add the carrots, potatoes, sweet potatoes, and tomatoes.
6. Add the bay leaves, thyme, and rosemary.
7. Season with salt and pepper to taste.
8. Pour in the beef stock and red wine.
9. Bring the potjie to a boil, then reduce the heat to low and let it simmer for 2-3 hours, or until the meat is tender.
10. Stir occasionally and add more stock or water if necessary to prevent the potjie from drying out.
11. Serve hot with some bread or rice.

Enjoy your delicious South African potjiekos!

Chicken & Veg Potjie

Ingredients:

8 chicken thighs
2 onions, chopped
2 cloves garlic, minced
2-3 carrots, sliced
2-3 potatoes, peeled and cubed
2-3 sweet potatoes, peeled and cubed
2-3 tomatoes, chopped
1 cup chicken stock
1 cup white wine
Salt and pepper
Olive oil

Instructions:

1. Heat some olive oil in your potjie pot over medium-high heat.
2. Add the chicken thighs and brown them on all sides.
3. Remove the chicken from the pot and set it aside.
4. Add a little more olive oil to the pot and then add the onions and garlic. Cook until the onions are translucent.
5. Add the carrots, potatoes, sweet potatoes, and tomatoes to the pot.
6. Season with salt and pepper to taste.
7. Pour in the chicken stock and white wine.
8. Bring the potjie to a boil, then reduce the heat to low and let it simmer for 1-2 hours, or until the chicken is cooked through and the vegetables are tender.
9. Stir occasionally and add more stock or water if necessary to prevent the potjie from drying out.
10. Serve hot with some bread or rice.

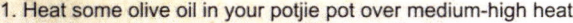

South African Potjiekos

Cowboy Potjie

Ingredients:

30ml *(2 tablespoons)* butter
30ml olive oil
2 onions, roughly chopped
500g ground beef
2 packs of bacon, chopped
10ml *(2 teaspoons)* chopped garlic
50ml brandy
10ml Aromat seasoning
5ml ground black pepper
10ml dried oregano
2 x 410g cans of beans in tomato sauce
410g chopped tomatoes with oregano and basil.
125ml freshly chopped parsley *(or half a teaspoon dried)*

Instructions:

1. Heat the butter and olive oil in a cast-iron pot over hot coals and sauté the onions until glossy.
2. Add the beef and stir-fry for 3 minutes.
3. Add the garlic, brandy, and seasonings and stir through.
4. Turn the cans of beans & tomatoes upside down and mix them in.
5. Put the lid on and heat it to boiling point over moderate coals.
6. Sprinkle the parsley on top and serve!

Lamb Stew Potjie

Ingredients:

100 ml (3.4 fl oz) oil
2 kg (4.4 lbs) lamb shanks
1/2 green bell pepper, chopped
1 large onion, chopped
2 garlic cloves, crushed
6 bacon rashers, rind removed, chopped
2 medium-sized tomatoes, chopped
2 beef stock cubes
Salt and black pepper to taste
250 ml (8.5 fl oz) white wine
250 ml (8.5 fl oz) boiling water
5 carrots, peeled and sliced
12 small potatoes, washed
5 baby marrows *(zucchini)*, sliced
400 g (14 oz) mushrooms

Instructions:

1. Heat the oil in a large cast-iron pot and brown the lamb shanks. The browner the meat, the richer the sauce will be.
2. Add the green pepper, onion, garlic, and bacon and sauté until the vegetables begin to brown.
3. Add the tomatoes and stir-fry for 5 minutes.
4. Add the beef stock, herbs, white wine, and boiling water, and simmer for an hour.
5. Add the carrots and potatoes, and simmer for 20 minutes. Lastly, add the baby marrows and mushrooms and simmer for a further 15 minutes. Add more liquid if necessary.

Tip: Do not stir the pot during the cooking process. Serve hot with rice, maize porridge, or bread.

Jan Braai Biltong Pasta Potjie

Ingredients:

250g (8.8 oz) biltong
500g (1.1 lb) pasta *(penne or shells)*
2 tablespoons olive oil
2 onions *(chopped)*
3 garlic cloves *(chopped)*
1 pack of bacon (200g/7 oz) cut into small cubes
250g (8.8 oz) mushrooms
1 beef stock cube
2 cups (500ml/16.9 fl oz) boiling water
1/2 cup (125ml/4.2 fl oz) white wine
1 pack (50g/1.8 oz) tomato paste
1 cup (250ml/8.5 fl oz) full cream milk
250g (8.8 oz) or more grated cheddar cheese
250ml (8.5 fl oz) fresh cream
salt and pepper to taste

Instructions:

1. Heat the oil in your potjie *(traditional South African cast-iron pot)* and fry the onions until they are translucent. Then add the garlic, bacon, and mushrooms and continue to fry until the bacon is cooked.
2. Dissolve the beef stock cube in 2 cups of boiling water and add it, along with the wine and tomato paste, to the potjie. Mix everything thoroughly.
3. Add the pasta and biltong. Stir everything well and put the lid on the pot. Let it simmer for 5 minutes and then remove the lid.
4. Stir in the milk, cheese, and cream. Let it simmer for 10-15min until the pasta is cooked and you are satisfied that the sauce is thick enough. Of course, you should check on it occasionally. If it becomes too dry and looks like it might burn, you can add a bit more water.
5. Once the pasta is cooked and you are satisfied that the sauce is thick enough, the meal is ready to be served.

Lamb Kidney Potjie

Ingredients:

50 ml (3.4 tbsp) oil
25 ml (1.7 tbsp) butter
3 large onions *(chopped)*
12 lamb kidneys *(sliced in half, with membranes/cores removed)*
50 ml (1/4 cup) cake flour
5 ml (1 tsp) salt
freshly ground black pepper
12.5 ml (2.5 tsp) tomato paste
200 ml (3/4 cup + 2 tbsp) chicken stock
50 ml (1/4 cup) dry white wine
8 pork sausages *(sliced in half)*
200 g (7 oz) mushrooms
50 ml (1/4 cup) brandy
12.5 ml (2.5 tsp) chopped parsley

Instructions:

1. Heat oil and butter in a three-legged pot over hot coals.
2. Add chopped onions and stir for 3 minutes.
3. Roll kidneys in a mixture of cake flour, salt, and pepper, and add to the onions in the pot.
4. Add all other ingredients except for brandy and parsley, and allow to cook over moderate coals without stirring.
5. When kidneys are cooked, add brandy and parsley, stir once and serve.

Potjiekos - South African Stew

Red Chicken Potjie

Ingredients:

Use a number 3 potjie
1 kg chicken (average weight of a normal chicken)
Fine Salt
Coarse Black Pepper
Flour for rolling chicken pieces in
2 medium onions, finely chopped
Cook rice separately until done
Ginger and Garlic (finely chopped) (2 teaspoons)

Ingredients for the Sauce:
Tomato Sauce (300ml) Koo brand
Chutney (50ml) Wellington brand
Worcestershire Sauce (20ml) Mrs. Balls brand
Tabasco Sauce (2ml)
Vinegar (50ml)
Sugar (50ml)
Mustard Powder (5ml)
Paprika (15ml) Robertson brand
Water (125ml)

Instructions:

Mix everything together in a bottle *(1 liter plastic Coke bottle)* and shake well to combine.

1. Heat your pot and add your butter (real) (20ml).
2. Fry the finely chopped onions and Ginger/Garlic (2 teaspoons) until fragrant.
3. Take the chicken portions and sprinkle each one individually with fine salt and pepper.
4. Dip the chicken portions in the flour add to the pot.
5. Stir until the chicken pieces are well coated with the onions and oil for about 10 minutes with the lid off. Use a wooden spoon. (The aroma will already make you hungry. From now on, don't stir your pot until you serve.)
6. Now add your sauce as assembled above and let your pot simmer. (Lightly bubbling throughout). Check the pot regularly for 15 minutes.
7. Now add your vegetables in layers in the following order: 10 small potatoes, 10 young carrots, 10 small type of pumpkin.
8. One pack "button" mushrooms to taste for the last 45min.
9. Add cooked rice about 10 minutes before serving and let the sauce simmer. The pot will take about 2 1/2 hours.
10. Get your wife to test the potatoes for doneness and ask her about the salt content. The different brands shown work best for me to bring out the taste.
11. Serve and enjoy the Red Chicken.

Blikpotjie

1 x large can of preserved food.

1. Open can, but not completely, so that the lid can be folded back as a covering when the pot is placed on fire.
2. Empty contents and keep or eat as preferred.

Place in empty can:
1/3 cup rice.
1 cup water
1/2 finely chopped onion.
1 small potato, diced *(optional)*
1/2 cup chopped vegetables *(carrots) (optional)*
salt
100 grams ground beef / bully beef *(finely sliced)*

3. Place can on fire and cook until rice is done.
4. Add water if necessary. Stir if necessary. 1 large meal for 1-2 people.

Chicken in Beer

Ingredients:

2 tbsp butter
1 tbsp cooking oil
125 g bacon, diced
2 chopped onions
2 chopped garlic cloves
1 chopped carrot
1 chopped celery stalk
1 chicken, cut into portions
1 tsp oregano
1 tsp salt
A few turns of the black pepper grinder
1 can of beer
3 handfuls of button mushrooms
1 generous handful of chopped fresh parsley

Instructions:

1. Heat your pot as explained here. Add butter and oil.
2. Fry bacon in the pot until it's nice and crispy brown, remove and set aside. Fry onion, garlic, carrot, and celery over the heat, scoop out and set aside.
3. Fry chicken until golden brown. Place pot on cooler coals that will provide heat for the rest of the cooking process.
4. Pour your bacon, onions, celery, carrot, and garlic back into the pot along with oregano, salt, and pepper.
5. Pour beer over the ingredients, put the lid on and make sure your vigilant simmering process begins.
6. Peek every so often but do not stir. Your chicken should be falling off the bone within an hour and a half. Add mushrooms and parsley, let simmer for another 15 minutes, and voila! *(Thicken the sauce if desired.)*

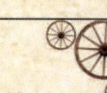

Venison Potjie

Ingredients:

1 kg (2.2 lb) cubed rooibok *(venison)* meat
4 yellow carrots, sliced
2 garlic cloves, finely crushed
250 g (8.8 oz) chopped bacon
6 potatoes, sliced
125 ml (1/2 cup) oil
2 onions, sliced
10 ml (2 tsp) chopped thyme
500 ml (2 cups) port or dry red wine

Instructions:

1. Heat oil in a cast iron pot and sauté yellow carrots, onions, and garlic until onions are translucent.
2. Add thyme, meat, bacon, and port. Simmer for 2 hours very slowly with lid on.
3. Add potatoes and simmer for another 30 to 45 minutes. Serve with mieliepap (maize meal porridge).

Blikpotjie

Beef Potjiekos

Beef Stew Potjie

Rich, meaty, and thick. It takes a nice long time to prepare and gives you the perfect opportunity to discover what potjiekos is really all about.

Ingredients:

3 tbsp cooking oil
1 beef tail, sliced
1 chopped onion
2 finely chopped garlic cloves
500ml dry red wine *(remember, if it's not good enough to drink, don't cook with it)*
2 bay leaves
2 teaspoons salt
1 tbsp dried rosemary
1 tbsp dried parsley
A few twists of black pepper
6 medium-sized carrots, peeled
4 celery stalks with leaves, cut into pieces
3 handfuls of fresh or frozen peas

Instructions:

1. Okay, now you get your pot nice and hot next to the fire or with a few flaming coals under it. If you throw in a few drops of wine and it sizzles clearly, the pot is hot. With the hot coals underneath, add your oil and brown the beef.
2. Then add your onions and stir the whole thing until the onions are translucent. Now place the pot away from the fire with just enough coals under its legs to keep it warm. Add everything except the carrots, celery, and peas.
3. Now it's time to test your pot management, because now the lid is going to be placed on the pot and it's going to stand for at least four to five hours. Keep your ear close to the pot. If everything bubbles, the coals are too hot - scrape them away.
4. You should hear a reassuring simmering and you should be able to hear "one thousand, two thousand" slowly between each bubble. You can occasionally lift the lid to see how things are going and give it a controlled stir.
5. After three hours, the meat should start to become tender, but don't hesitate to push it towards four hours. Make sure your coals are still warm. About 20 to 30 minutes before your meat reaches its desired tenderness, lift the lid. The smell should knock you over.
6. Now you pack your carrots, celery, and peas on top of the beef, put the lid back on. Don't stir anymore and remove the pot when the carrots are tender.

TIP: There's going to be a delicious sauce, but some people like a thick sauce. In that case, add two to three handfuls of breadcrumbs or half a packet of onion soup. It works wonders. Serve with rice or mashed potatoes.

Potjiekos

Biltong Potjie

Biltong potjie is a very quick and delicious dish that doesn't require any thawing... hope the biltong hasn't been eaten yet!

Ingredients:

6 onions, chopped
5 packs (1.25 kg/2.75 lb total) of mushrooms or 5 cans (205 g/7.2 oz each) of creamed mushrooms
1 kg/2.2 lb biltong
5 cans (418 g/14.7 oz each) of whole kernel corn or creamed sweet corn
5 packs of noodles (cooked)
2 green peppers, sliced
5 packs of white or cheese sauce, mixed with boiling water *(5 boxes of long-life cream can also be used instead of sauce)*
5 cups of grated cheddar *(optional)*

Instructions:

1. Fry onions and mushrooms. Add green pepper, corn, and biltong. Add cooked noodles. Pour sauce or cream over it. Add cheese on top.
2. Keep the pot on low heat until the cheese has melted.
3. Another piece of advice is not to mix too much with the ingredients in the pot, otherwise, you will end up with a mushy dish. Cook the meat first, then add the vegetables in layers. Then give it a quick stir before serving over rice or mashed potatoes.
4. But let's get to the food. (All recipes are for a number 3 tripod pot and are more or less enough for six people. Remember that the pot should never be more than three-quarters full, otherwise, there won't be enough steam to cook everything.)

Seafood Potjie

Ingredients:

500g (1.1 lbs) mixed seafood *(prawns, mussels, calamari, fish fillets)*
2 tablespoons vegetable oil
1 onion, finely chopped
2 garlic cloves, minced
2 carrots, peeled and diced
2 potatoes, peeled and diced
1 red bell pepper, diced
1 can diced tomatoes
240ml (1 cup) fish or vegetable stock
1 teaspoon paprika
1 teaspoon dried thyme
1 teaspoon dried oregano
Salt and pepper to taste
Fresh parsley, chopped (for garnish)
Lemon wedges (for serving)

Instructions:

1. Heat the vegetable oil in a large potjie pot or heavy-bottomed pot over medium heat.
2. Add the chopped onion and minced garlic to the pot and sauté until softened and fragrant.
3. Add the diced carrots, potatoes, and red bell pepper to the pot and cook for a few minutes until slightly tender.
4. Stir in the diced tomatoes, fish or vegetable stock, paprika, dried thyme, and dried oregano. Season with salt and pepper to taste.
5. Bring the mixture to a simmer and let it cook for about 10 minutes, allowing the flavors to meld together.
6. Add the mixed seafood to the pot, ensuring it is evenly distributed. Cover the pot with a lid and let it simmer for another 10-15 minutes or until the seafood is cooked through.
7. Taste and adjust the seasoning if needed.
8. Remove from heat and garnish with freshly chopped parsley.
9. Serve the Seafood Potjie hot with lemon wedges on the side.

Beef Stew Potjiekos

Breakfast Potjie

Ingredients:

Leftover braaied meat, cut into cubes
Onions
Can of tomato sauce
Minced meat
Chopped bacon
Green pepper
Mushrooms
Small can of baked beans in tomato sauce
Eggs
Cheese
Anything else you like

Instructions:

1. Fry onions, green pepper, and mushrooms. Add meat and fry.
2. Add tomato sauce and baked beans and let it simmer. Season with salt, pepper, and spices.
3. Break eggs on top and cover to cook. Sprinkle grated cheese on top and serve on a bread roll or any leftover starch that is available.
4. Any combination of ingredients can be used to prevent the waste of leftover braaied meat.
5. Basically, anything you like can be used.

Biltong Potjie — (Serves 10)

Ingredients:

3 chopped onions
1 chopped red pepper
1 chopped green pepper
1 can of pineapple
1 package of savory rice
1 kg/2.2 lb raw rice
1 package of "spice up your rice".
1 can of whole kernel corn
500 g/1.1 lb of sliced biltong
1 package of small button mushrooms
1 can of carrot chunks
250 g/8.8 oz of grated cheese

Instructions:

1. Fry onions, red, and green peppers. Mix rice with savory rice and spice up your rice.
2. Mix with 2 liters of water and add raw rice to the pot. Simmer rice until soft and cooked.
3. Add corn, carrots, and pineapple. Pineapple sauce can also be added to the pot. Cook for 20minutes and add mushrooms. Cook for another 15 minutes until cooked.
4. When the rice is soft, stir in the biltong and add grated cheese on top of the rice mixture.
5. Cover for 5min for the cheese to melt. Serve and enjoy.

Instructions:

Fry onions and mushrooms. Add green peppers, corn, and biltong. Add cooked noodles. Pour sauce or cream over it. Sprinkle grated cheese on top. Keep the pot on low heat until the cheese is melted. Do not mix the ingredients too much, or the dish will become mushy. Cook the meat until tender, then add the vegetables in layers. Give it a quick stir before serving over rice or mashed potatoes.

Note that the pot should never be more than three-quarters full, or there will not be enough steam to cook everything.

Chicken Biltong & Bacon Potjie

Ingredients:

Sauce:
2 chicken stock cubes
250 ml (1 cup) boiling water
500 ml (2 cups) dry white wine
250 ml (1 cup) chutney
46 g mushroom soup powder *(1 packet)*
5 ml (1 tsp) dried thyme
5 ml (1 tsp) mixed dried herbs
5 ml (1 tsp) lemon pepper

Chicken Dish:
15 ml (1 tbsp) olive oil
15 ml (1 tbsp) butter
12 chicken thighs, skin removed if preferred
250 g bacon, chopped *(1 packet)*
50 ml brandy
10 ml (2 tsp) chopped garlic - optional
2 onions, sliced into rings
1/2 green bell pepper, roughly chopped
1 celery stalk, thinly sliced
20 small potatoes, peeled
4 carrots, sliced into rounds
12 small onions, whole
250 g button mushrooms
8 marrow squash, sliced into thick rounds
150 g moist beef biltong, sliced
250 ml (1 cup) grated Cheddar cheese
125 ml (1/2 cup) fresh chopped parsley

Instructions:

Sauce:
1. Dissolve the stock cubes in the boiling water.
2. Mix the rest of the ingredients for the sauce and add it to the stock.
3. Set the sauce aside.

Chicken Dish:
1. Heat the butter and oil over medium heat and brown the chicken.
2. Add the bacon and sauté for 3 minutes. Add the brandy and garlic. Stir and do not stir again.
3. Sprinkle the onions, bell pepper, and celery over the chicken and place the potatoes and carrots on top.
4. Pour the sauce over: Place the lid on and let it simmer for 1 hour. Add boiling water if necessary.
5. Cover and simmer for 20 minutes. Stir just before serving and sprinkle with parsley.

Biltong Potjie — (Biltong Stew)

Biltong Potjie is a quick and delicious dish that requires no thawing time. The recipe serves six people and is cooked in a pot over low heat.

Ingredients:

6 onions, sliced
5 packs of 250g mushrooms or
5 cans of 410g creamy mushrooms
1 kg biltong *(dried meat)*
5 cans of creamed corn
5 packs of cooked noodles
2 green peppers, sliced
5 packs of white or
cheese sauce, made with boiling water *(5 boxes of long-life cream can be used instead of the sauce)*
5 cups grated cheddar cheese *(optional)*

Tomato Bredie

This is a traditional South African recipe.

Ingredients:

25 ml (1.7 tbsp) butter or margarine
2 large onions, chopped
1 garlic clove, crushed
1.5 kg (3.3 lb) lamb or mutton, cubed
10 ml (2 tsp) salt
some stock, water or wine
500 g (1.1 lb) potatoes, sliced
1 kg (2.2 lb) medium tomatoes, peeled and chopped
5 ml (1 tsp) white sugar
2 ml (0.4 tsp) dried thyme
5 ml (1 tsp) chopped fresh marjoram

Instructions:

1. Heat the butter in a pot and fry the onions and garlic for about 5 minutes or until the onions are translucent. Add the meat and quickly fry until brown on all sides. Add salt, pepper, and a little bit of the stock, water, or wine, cover, and simmer for 90 to 120min or until the meat starts to become tender.
2. Add the potatoes, tomatoes, sugar, thyme, and marjoram and cook for another hour.
3. Serve with rice.

Tribe Stew

Ingredients:

2 pieces of sheep's tripe *(well cleaned)*
Water for boiling
250 ml *(1 cup)* of semi-sweet white wine
Juice of 1/2 lemon
Salt and freshly ground black pepper
1 sheep neck
6 large onions *(chopped)*
12 small potatoes
25 ml *(5 tsp)* of med strength curry powder
2 ml *(1/2 tsp)* of chili powder
10 ml *(2 tsp)* of dark brown sugar
Vinegar for seasoning
250 g *(9 oz)* of dried apricots

Instructions:

1. Cut the tripe into cubes and place in a three-legged pot with water, wine, lemon juice, salt, pepper, and sheep neck.
2. Cover the pot, place it over medium heat and let it cook until the contents are tender, approximately 3-4 hours.
3. When the tripe cubes are tender and the meat falls off the neck bones, remove the neck bones, add onions and potatoes to the pot and cook for another 30 minutes.
4. Mix curry powder, chili powder, and sugar with vinegar and add together with apricots to the pot. Cover and place back on heat for another 30 minutes. Stir well and serve.

Fish Blitz Pot

This recipe employs a different technique, namely more heat and less time. The recipe is derived from one of the many versions of the French fish soup/stew known as bouillabaisse, but it tastes better alongside a piece of South African coast than in any European cafe.

Ingredients:

2 finely chopped onions
1 kg to 1.2 kg (2.2 to 2.6 lb) fresh firm fish *(yellowtail, kingklip, yellowtail, cod)* cut into pieces that will fit into a tablespoon.
4 finely chopped garlic cloves
3 cans of tomatoes, finely chopped
¾ cup of olive oil
1 tsp of dried fennel
Zest of half a lemon *(pref. sun-dried & cut into small pieces.)*
a handful of freshly chopped parsley
2 pinches of saffron

Instructions:

1. Get your pot, fire and guests ready because this dish will be ready within 20 minutes. Heat the pot, add a spoonful of olive oil to the warm pot and fry your onions until they are translucent.
2. Now place the pot on a good pile of hot coals and, believe it or not, throw all the ingredients except parsley and saffron into the pot.
3. Stir quickly because the olive oil is the binder in which everything will cook - no wine or lemon juice that will break the oil's effect.
4. When the pot starts to boil well, place the lid on, wait for 12 to 15 minutes, sprinkle parsley and saffron over everything and serve in soup bowls.
5. Delicious with rice, but especially delicious on thick slices of toasted bread.

Hearty Potjiekos

Notes

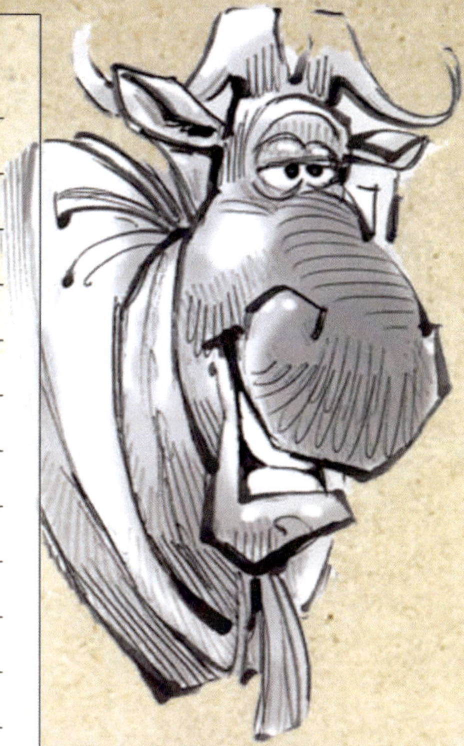

_____
_____
_____
_____
_____
_____
_____
_____
_____
_____
_____
_____
_____
_____

Notes

_____
_____
_____
_____
_____
_____
_____
_____
_____
_____
_____
_____
_____
_____
_____
_____
_____

The Unforgettable words of Susanna

A Tale of Defiance and Determination

Similar to the emergence of Wolraad Woltemade or Dirkie Uys from obscurity, who immortalized themselves in our history through acts of bravery, Susanna Smit will forever inspire the Afrikaans people. Her greatest accomplishment was stepping forward and uttering a word that would echo through the ages as a refrain in a freedom song.

She epitomized the unwavering determination of the Afrikaner to be free from foreign domination. Though little is known about her life, Susanna Smit, born on August 28th, 1798, and passing away on July 27th, 1863, in Pietermaritzburg, held a significant position as the sister of Voortrekker leader Gert Maritz and the wife of the first Voortrekker (*Pioneers*) minister, Reverend Erasmus Smit. Among the women of the Voortrekkers (*Pioneers*), she was revered.

Susanna Smit endured the trials and tribulations of the Voortrekkers (*Pioneers*) in the Free State and Natal, and she continued to act as a leader and spokesperson for the women of the trekker community while being the wife of a minister. This is evident from the fact that she was chosen as the spokesperson for a delegation of approximately 400 dissatisfied women who protested against the annexation of Natal by the English, advocating for Cloete, the representative sent by the British government to take over the land. It was during this occasion that Susanna Smit secured a lasting place in our historical records.

The women invited Cloete to meet them in the courthouse, which served as the meeting place for the Volksraad. As the leader of the delegation, Susanna Smit eloquently conveyed the reasons why they had left the Cape Colony and the hardships and oppression they had endured to secure their land. She made it unequivocally clear that accepting the British annexation plans was impossible for them.

When Cloete grew impatient and refused to listen further, Susanna Smit expressed, with even greater force, the unwavering determination of her people to never submit to British rule. With profound passion, she declared, "Mr. Cloete, all the pretty promises made here taste like aloes in our mouths. We have shed our blood and sweat to escape the despised British flag, and even if we have to walk barefoot and bareheaded over the Drakensberg, we will not surrender under that flag."

And then she vanished from the scene. However, her words continued to reverberate and gain strength: "freedom or death" – an embodiment of the indomitable will and determination of Afrikaans women and the Afrikaans people. Each time these words were repeated, the figure of Susanna Smit came back to life.

Although she did not boast of great deeds, she became a folk figure, a true inspiration whose name will forever be mentioned wherever South African history is proclaimed.

"Liewer kaalvoet terug oor die Drakensberge as om onder Britse beheer te staan."

("Rather barefoot back over the Drakensberg mountains than to be under British control.")

Soups & Stews

Sweet Potato Soup

Ingredients:

1 tablespoon olive oil (15 ml)
1 onion, chopped (150 g / 5.3 oz)
2 cloves garlic, minced
2 carrots, peeled and chopped (150 g / 5.3 oz)
2 celery stalks, chopped (150 g / 5.3 oz)
1 sweet potato, peeled and chopped (300 g / 10.6 oz)
1 can diced tomatoes (400 g / 14 oz)
4 cups vegetable broth (1 liter)
1 teaspoon dried thyme (5 g / 0.2 oz)
1 teaspoon dried oregano (5 g / 0.2 oz)
Salt and pepper to taste

Instructions:

1. Heat the olive oil in a Dutch oven over medium heat. Add the onion and garlic and cook until the onion is soft and translucent, about 5 minutes.
2. Add the carrots, celery, & sweet potato and cook for another 5min.
3. Add the diced tomatoes, vegetable broth, thyme, and oregano. Season with salt and pepper to taste.
4. Bring the soup to a boil, then reduce the heat and simmer for 20-25 minutes, until the vegetables are tender.
5. Use an immersion blender or transfer the soup to a blender and blend until smooth.
6. Taste and adjust seasoning as needed. Serve hot.

Beef Stew

Ingredients:

1 kg (2.2 lb) beef chuck, cut into cubes
2 tablespoons flour (20 g)
2 tablespoons olive oil (30 ml)
1 onion, chopped (150 g / 5.3 oz)
2 cloves garlic, minced
2 carrots, peeled and chopped (150 g / 5.3 oz)
2 celery stalks, chopped (150 g / 5.3 oz)
2 potatoes, peeled and cut into chunks (300 g / 10.6 oz)
1 tablespoon tomato paste (15 g)
500 ml (2 cups) beef broth
1 bay leaf
1 teaspoon dried thyme (5 g / 0.2 oz)
Salt and pepper to taste

Instructions:

1. Toss the beef cubes with the flour until they are coated.
2. Heat the olive oil in a Dutch oven over medium-high heat. Add the beef and cook until browned on all sides, about 5-7 minutes.
3. Add the onion and garlic to the pot and cook until the onion is soft and translucent, about 5 minutes.
4. Add the carrots, celery, and potatoes, and cook for another 5min.
5. Add the tomato paste, beef broth, bay leaf, thyme, and season with salt and pepper to taste.
6. Bring the stew to a boil, then reduce the heat to low and let it simmer for about 2 hours, until the beef is tender.
7. Remove the bay leaf and discard.
8. Taste and adjust seasoning as needed. Serve hot.

Mushroom Risotto

Ingredients:

1 tablespoon olive oil (15 ml)
1 tablespoon butter (15 g)
1 onion, finely chopped (150 g / 5.3 oz)
2 garlic cloves, minced
300 g (10.6 oz) Arborio rice
150 ml (2/3 cup) dry white wine
900 ml (3 3/4 cups) hot vegetable or chicken broth
250 g (8.8 oz) mushrooms, sliced
50 g (1.8 oz) grated Parmesan cheese
Salt and pepper to taste

Instructions:

1. Heat the olive oil and butter in a large Dutch oven or heavy-bottomed pot over medium heat.
2. Add the onion and garlic and cook until the onion is soft and translucent, about 5 minutes.
3. Add the Arborio rice and stir until it is coated in the oil and butter.
4. Pour in the white wine and cook, stirring constantly, until it is absorbed by the rice.
5. Add the hot broth, one ladleful at a time, stirring constantly and waiting until each ladleful is absorbed before adding the next.
6. After about 10 minutes, add the sliced mushrooms and continue to add the broth as before.
7. Keep stirring the risotto for about 18-20 minutes in total, or until the rice is cooked but still has a bit of bite.
8. Turn off the heat, stir in the grated Parmesan cheese, and season with salt and pepper to taste.
9. Let the risotto rest for a couple of minutes before serving.

Lentil Soup

Ingredients:

2 tablespoons olive oil (30 ml)
1 onion, chopped (150 g / 5.3 oz)
2 cloves garlic, minced
2 carrots, peeled and chopped (150 g / 5.3 oz)
2 celery stalks, chopped (150 g / 5.3 oz)
1 cup brown lentils, rinsed (200 g)
1 can diced tomatoes (400 g / 14 oz)
4 cups vegetable broth (1 lite)
1 teaspoon cumin powder (5 g / 0.2 oz)
1/2 teaspoon paprika (2.5 g / 0.1 oz)
Salt and pepper to taste
1 lemon, cut into wedges

Instructions:

1. Heat the olive oil in a Dutch oven over medium-high heat. Add the onion and garlic and cook until the onion is soft and translucent, about 5 minutes.
2. Add the carrots and celery and cook for another 5 minutes.
3. Add the lentils, canned tomatoes, vegetable broth, cumin powder, paprika, and season with salt and pepper to taste.
4. Bring the soup to a boil, then reduce the heat to low and let it simmer for about 30-40 minutes, until the lentils are tender.
5. Taste and adjust seasoning as needed.
6. Serve hot with a wedge of lemon.

Sweet Potato Soup

Beef Stroganoff

Ingredients:

1 pound beef sirloin, sliced into thin strips (450 g)
2 tablespoons all-purpose flour (16 g / 0.5 oz)
1/2 teaspoon salt (2.5 g / 0.1 oz)
1/2 teaspoon black pepper (2.5 g / 0.1 oz)
2 tablespoons butter (28 g / 1 oz)
1 onion, chopped (150 g / 5.3 oz)
2 cloves garlic, minced
8 ounces sliced mushrooms (225 g)
1 tablespoon tomato paste (15 g / 0.5 oz)
1 1/2 cups beef broth (360 ml)
1/2 cup sour cream (120 ml)
1/4 cup chopped fresh parsley (15 g / 0.5 oz)
12 ounces egg noodles (340 g)

Instructions:

1. Combine the flour, salt, and black pepper in a shallow dish. Coat the beef strips in the mixture.
2. Heat the butter in a Dutch oven over medium-high heat. Add the onion and garlic and cook until the onion is soft and translucent, about 5 minutes.
3. Add the beef and cook until browned on all sides, about 5-7min.
4. Add the mushrooms and cook for another 5 minutes.
5. Stir in the tomato paste and beef broth. Bring to a simmer and cook for about 10-15 minutes, until the sauce has thickened.
6. Meanwhile, cook the egg noodles according to package instructions.
7. Remove the Dutch oven from heat and stir in the sour cream and parsley.
8. Serve the beef stroganoff over the cooked egg noodles.

Chickpea Soup

Ingredients:

1 tablespoon (15ml) olive oil
1 onion, chopped (about 1 cup or 150g)
2 garlic cloves, minced
3 carrots, chopped (about 2 cups or 300g)
2 celery stalks, chopped (about 1 cup or 150g)
1 teaspoon dried thyme
1 teaspoon dried oregano
1 teaspoon smoked paprika
1/2 teaspoon salt
1/4 teaspoon black pepper
6 cups (1.4L) chicken or vegetable broth
1 can (14oz or 400g) diced tomatoes, undrained
1 cup (170g) uncooked quinoa
1 can (14oz or 400g) chickpeas, drained and rinsed
1/4 cup (10g) chopped fresh parsley
2 tablespoons (30ml) freshly squeezed lemon juice

Instructions:

1. Heat the olive oil in a Dutch oven over medium heat. Add the onion and garlic and cook +- 5min until the onion is translucent.
2. Add the carrots and celery and cook for another 5 minutes, until the vegetables are slightly softened.
3. Stir in the thyme, oregano, smoked paprika, salt, and pepper.
4. Add the broth and diced tomatoes and bring to a boil.
5. Stir in the quinoa and chickpeas and reduce heat to low. Cover and simmer for 20-25 minutes, or until the quinoa is cooked and the vegetables are tender.
6. Stir in the chopped parsley and lemon juice. Adjust seasonings to taste.
7. Serve hot, garnished with additional fresh parsley if desired.

Whole Chicken

Ingredients:

1 whole chicken (3 to 4 pounds / 1.4 to 1.8kg)
2 tablespoons (30g) butter, softened
1 tablespoon (15ml) olive oil
2 teaspoons (10g) salt
1 teaspoon (5g) black pepper
1 teaspoon (5g) paprika
1 teaspoon (5g) garlic powder
1 onion, chopped
2 carrots, chopped
2 celery stalks, chopped
1 lemon, sliced
1 cup (240ml) chicken broth
Fresh parsley, chopped *(optional)*

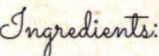

Instructions:

1. Preheat the oven to 400°F (200°C).
2. In a small bowl, combine the softened butter, olive oil, salt, black pepper, paprika, and garlic powder.
3. Place the chicken in the Dutch oven and spread the butter mixture over the chicken, making sure to coat it evenly.
4. Add the chopped onion, carrots, celery, and lemon slices to the Dutch oven, around the chicken.
5. Pour the chicken broth into the Dutch oven.
6. Cover the Dutch oven and bake in the preheated oven for 1 hour and 30 minutes to 2 hours, or until the chicken is cooked through (internal temperature should be 165°F / 75°C).
7. Remove the chicken from the Dutch oven and let it rest for 10min. before carving.
8. Serve the chicken with the vegetables and broth, garnished with fresh parsley, if desired.

Lemon Garlic Chicken

Ingredients:

4 bone-in chicken thighs
1 lemon, sliced
4 cloves garlic, minced
2 tbsp olive oil
1 tbsp honey
1 tsp dried oregano
1 tsp salt
1/2 tsp black pepper
Fresh parsley, chopped *(optional)*

Instructions:

1. Preheat the oven to 200°C (400°F).
2. In a small bowl, whisk together the minced garlic, olive oil, honey, dried oregano, salt, and black pepper.
3. Place the thighs on a baking sheet lined with parchment paper.
4. Brush the garlic mixture generously over the chicken thighs, making sure to coat all sides.
5. Place a few slices of lemon on top of each chicken thigh.
6. Bake in the preheated oven for 30-35 minutes or until the internal temperature of the chicken reaches 75°C (165°F).
7. Remove from the oven and let the chicken rest for 5 minutes before serving.
8. Garnish with chopped parsley, if desired.

Beef Stroganoff

Pot Roast

Ingredients:

3 lb (1.4 kg) beef chuck roast
1 tbsp (15 ml) vegetable oil
1 large onion, chopped
2 cloves garlic, minced
1 tsp (5 ml) dried thyme
2 bay leaves
2 cups (480 ml) beef broth
4 medium carrots, peeled and chopped
4 medium potatoes, peeled and chopped
Salt and pepper to taste

Instructions:

1. Preheat the oven to 325°F (160°C).
2. Heat the oil in a Dutch oven over medium-high heat.
3. Season the beef with salt and pepper and brown it on all sides in the Dutch oven. Remove the beef and set it aside.
4. Add the onion and garlic to the Dutch oven and sauté until softened, about 5 minutes.
5. Add the thyme and bay leaves and cook for another minute.
6. Add the beef broth to the Dutch oven and stir to scrape up any browned bits on the bottom of the pan.
7. Return the beef to the Dutch oven, cover with the lid, and place it in the oven.
8. Bake for 2 hours, then add the chopped carrots and potatoes to the Dutch oven.
9. Cover the Dutch oven again and bake for another hour or until the vegetables are tender and the beef is fork-tender.
10. Remove the Dutch oven from the oven and let it rest for a few minutes before serving.

Chicken & Dumplings

Ingredients:

1 whole chicken, about 3 pounds (1.4kg)
2 tablespoons (30g) unsalted butter
2 tablespoons (30ml) olive oil
1 onion, chopped
3 celery stalks, chopped
3 carrots, peeled and chopped
4 garlic cloves, minced
1 teaspoon (5g) salt
1/2 teaspoon (2.5g) black pepper
8 cups (1.9L) chicken broth
2 cups (240g) all-purpose flour
1 tablespoon (15g) baking powder
1 teaspoon (5g) salt
1/2 teaspoon (2.5g) black pepper
1/2 cup (120ml) milk
1/4 cup (60g) unsalted butter, melted
2 tablespoons (30g) chopped fresh parsley

Instructions:

1. Preheat the oven to 350°F (180°C).
2. In a Dutch oven, melt the butter with the olive oil over med heat.
3. Add the chopped onion, celery, and carrots to the Dutch oven and cook until softened, about 5 minutes.
4. Add the minced garlic, salt, and black pepper to the Dutch oven and cook for another minute.
5. Add the whole chicken to the Dutch oven, breast side up, and pour the chicken broth over it. Bring to a boil, then reduce the heat to low and cover the Dutch oven with a lid.

Baked Beans

Ingredients:

1 pound (450g) dried navy beans
1 onion, chopped
1/2 cup (120ml) ketchup
1/2 cup (120ml) molasses
1/4 cup (60ml) apple cider vinegar
2 tablespoons (30ml) Worcestershire sauce
1 tablespoon (15ml) Dijon mustard
1 tablespoon (15ml) smoked paprika
1 teaspoon (5g) salt
1/2 teaspoon (2.5g) black pepper
4 cups (960ml) water
1/4 pound (110g) bacon, chopped
1/4 cup (60g) brown sugar
1 tablespoon (15ml) vegetable oil

Instructions:

1. Soak the dried navy beans in water overnight.
2. Preheat the oven to 300°F (150°C).
3. In a Dutch oven, heat the vegetable oil over medium-high heat.
4. Add the chopped bacon to the Dutch oven and cook until crispy, about 5 minutes.
5. Add the chopped onion to the Dutch oven and cook until softened, about 5 minutes.
6. Drain the soaked navy beans and add them to the Dutch oven.
7. Add the ketchup, molasses, apple cider vinegar, Worcestershire sauce, Dijon mustard, smoked paprika, salt, black pepper, and water to the Dutch oven. Stir to combine.
8. Cover the Dutch oven and transfer it to the preheated oven. Bake for 4 to 5 hours, or until the navy beans are tender and the liquid has thickened.
9. Stir in the brown sugar & continue baking for an additional 30min.
10. Remove the Dutch oven from the oven and let it cool for a few minutes before serving.

Baked Chicken & Dumplings

6. Transfer the Dutch oven to the preheated oven and bake for 1 to 1 1/2 hours, or until the chicken is cooked through and tender.
7. Remove the chicken from the Dutch oven and let it cool slightly. Remove the skin and bones from the chicken and shred the meat. Return the shredded chicken to the Dutch oven.
8. In a mixing bowl, whisk together the all-purpose flour, baking powder, salt, and black pepper.
9. Add the milk and melted butter to the mixing bowl and stir until a dough forms.
10. Drop spoonfuls of the dough onto the chicken mixture in the Dutch oven. Cover the Dutch oven and simmer for 20 to 30 minutes, or until the dumplings are cooked through.
11. Sprinkle the chopped fresh parsley over the chicken and dumplings before serving.

Notes

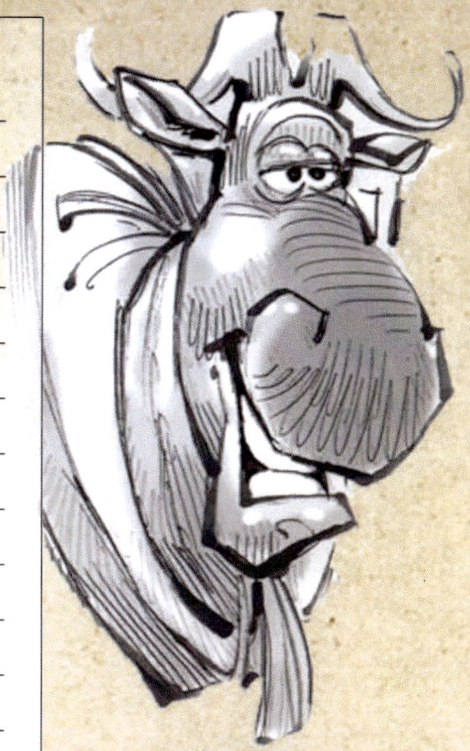

_____
_____
_____
_____
_____
_____
_____
_____
_____
_____
_____
_____
_____
_____
_____
_____
_____

Notes

_____
_____
_____
_____
_____
_____
_____
_____
_____
_____
_____
_____
_____
_____
_____
_____
_____

Spirit of The Boers

A Story of Courage and Resilience

The scorching sun relentlessly beat down on the vast plains of the Highveld, baking the earth until it cracked like weathered leather. A group of Voortrekker pioneers, led by a man named Willem, trudged wearily through the dust, the oxen straining under the weight of their wagons. It had been a long and difficult journey, and they had faced many dangers along the way. Despite the numerous dangers they faced, their determination to reach the promised land, known as the Transvaal, never wavered.

Across the endless grasslands, Willem regaled his fellow pioneers with stories of the brave Boers who had gone before them. Tales of Piet Retief and Andries Pretorius resonated, narrating victories against the formidable Zulu armies. He recounted the epic trek over the Drakensberg Mountains, the battles fought against the Matabele and the Basuto, and the immense hardships and sacrifices made to secure a place for the Boers in this harsh and unforgiving land. These stories also foretold of future struggles for freedom and independence, including wars against the British Empire.

Listening intently, the pioneers absorbed Willem's narratives, their eyes shining with pride and determination. They understood that they were the custodians of a grand legacy, entrusted with carrying forward the Boer traditions of courage, self-sufficiency, and independence. Approaching the banks of the Vaal River, they paused to rest and replenish their supplies. Gathered around the campfire, Willem shared one final story—a tale of a man named Paul Kruger, who would later become the president of the Transvaal Republic.

Willem recounted Kruger's childhood in the rugged wilderness of the bushveld, highlighting his bravery and skills as a hunter and warrior, as well as his profound love for his people and his land. He spoke of the day when Kruger, aged and frail, would be compelled to flee his beloved Transvaal, surrounded by the armies of the British Empire. Yet, Willem emphasized that even in exile, Kruger never lost faith in the destiny of his people. He carried the stories of the Boers who had paved the way before him—their struggles and sacrifices to carve out a place for their descendants in this challenging yet magnificent land.

As the pioneers absorbed Willem's words, a profound sense of awe and inspiration enveloped them. They realized that their journey had only just begun, with countless challenges and hardships ahead. However, they also recognized that they carried within them the indomitable spirit of the Boers who had gone before—those who had forged a path and left an enduring legacy. With each step on this momentous and perilous journey, they vowed to honour that legacy and uphold the spirit of the Boers who had shaped their destiny.

Dried Delights

The purpose of drying fruit is to extend its shelf life, making it last longer than fresh fruit.

The process of drying fruit removes most of the water content, which slows down the growth of microorganisms that cause spoilage. As a result, dried fruit can be stored for longer periods of time without the need for refrigeration or other preservation methods.

Dried fruit is also a convenient and portable snack that can be enjoyed on the go. Additionally, some people prefer the taste and texture of dried fruit over fresh fruit, and it can be used in a variety of recipes, such as baked goods, trail mixes, and salads. Finally, dried fruit can be a good source of vitamins, minerals, and fiber, making it a healthy addition to your diet in moderation.

To make dried fruit, you typically need fresh fruit, a knife, and either an oven or a food dehydrator. Here are the general steps for drying fruit:

- Select ripe, fresh fruit.
- Wash the fruit in cool water and pat it dry.
- Cut the fruit into thin slices or small pieces, removing any pits or seeds.
- Arrange the fruit pieces in a single layer on a baking sheet or in a food dehydrator tray.
- If using an oven, preheat it to the lowest possible temperature (usually around 140-170°F or 60-75°C). If using a dehydrator, follow the manufacturer's instructions.
- Place the baking sheet or dehydrator tray in the oven or dehydrator.
- Dry the fruit for several hours, rotating the trays occasionally, until the fruit is dry and slightly leathery or crispy. The drying time will vary depending on the type of fruit, its thickness, and the drying method.
- Once the fruit is fully dried, remove it from the oven or dehydrator and allow it to cool completely.
- Store the dried fruit in an airtight container at room temperature for up to several months.

Dried Fruit Salad

Ingredients:

1 cup dried apricots
1 cup raisins
1 cup prunes
1 cup dried apples
1 cup dried pears
1 cup dried peaches
1 cup dried figs
1 cup dried cranberries
1 cup fresh orange juice
1 cup water
1 cinnamon stick
1/2 cup sugar
2 tablespoons lemon juice

Instructions:

1. In a large pot, combine the dried fruit, orange juice, water, cinnamon stick, and sugar.
2. Bring the mixture to a boil over medium-high heat, stirring occasionally.
3. Reduce the heat to low and simmer for 20-30 minutes or until the fruit is tender and the liquid has thickened.
4. Remove the pot from the heat and stir in the lemon juice.
5. Let the fruit mixture cool completely, then transfer to a large bowl.
6. Cover the bowl with plastic wrap and refrigerate for at least 4 hours or overnight.
7. Serve the chilled dried fruit salad as a snack or use it as a topping for yogurt or ice cream.

Biltong & Dried Fruit Snack Mix

Ingredients:

1 cup biltong (dried meat)
1 cup mixed dried fruit (apricots, peaches, figs, etc.)
1 cup salted peanuts
1 cup pretzel sticks
1/2 cup raisins
1/2 cup roasted almonds
1/2 teaspoon smoked paprika
1/2 teaspoon garlic powder
1/2 teaspoon onion powder
1/4 teaspoon cayenne pepper
Salt and black pepper to taste

Instructions:

1. In a large bowl, combine the biltong, mixed dried fruit, peanuts, pretzel sticks, raisins, and roasted almonds.
2. In a small bowl, mix together the smoked paprika, garlic powder, onion powder, cayenne pepper, salt, and black pepper.
3. Sprinkle the spice mixture over the snack mix and toss well to coat.
4. Transfer the snack mix to an airtight container and store at room temperature for up to 1 week.
5. Serve the biltong and dried fruit snack mix as a savory and satisfying snack.

Dried Bananas

Ingredients:

Ripe bananas
Lemon juice or citric acid (optional)

Instructions:

1. Preheat your oven to 170°F (or the lowest temperature setting). If using a dehydrator, set it to 135°F.
2. Peel the bananas and slice them into uniform pieces, about ¼ inch thick.
3. If you want to prevent the bananas from browning, dip them in a solution of lemon juice or citric acid and water (1 tablespoon of lemon juice or citric acid to 1 cup of water).
4. Arrange the banana slices in a single layer on a baking sheet or dehydrator tray. Make sure there is some space between each slice to allow for air circulation.
5. Place the banana slices in the oven or dehydrator and let them dry for 6 to 8 hours. Check the bananas periodically and flip them over to ensure even drying.
6. The bananas are done when they are completely dry and slightly chewy. They should not feel sticky or moist.
7. Remove the dried bananas from the oven or dehydrator and let them cool completely.
8. Store the dried bananas in an airtight container at room temperature for up to a month. You can also store them in the refrigerator or freezer for longer shelf life.

Enjoy your homemade dried bananas as a snack, in cereal, or use them in baking recipes.

Dried Apricots

Ingredients:

Fresh apricots
Lemon juice or citric acid (optional)

Instructions:

1. Preheat your oven to 170°F (or the lowest temperature setting). If using a dehydrator, set it to 135°F.
2. Wash the apricots and cut them in half, removing the pits.
3. If you want to prevent the apricots from browning, dip them in a solution of lemon juice or citric acid and water (1 tablespoon of lemon juice or citric acid to 1 cup of water).
4. Arrange the apricot halves in a single layer on a baking sheet or dehydrator tray. Make sure there is some space between each piece to allow for air circulation.
5. Place the apricots in the oven or dehydrator and let them dry for 8 to 12 hours. Check the apricots periodically and flip them over to ensure even drying.
6. The apricots are done when they are completely dry and slightly chewy. They should not feel sticky or moist.
7. Remove the dried apricots from the oven or dehydrator and let them cool completely.
8. Store the dried apricots in an airtight container at room temperature for up to a month. You can also store them in the refrigerator or freezer for longer shelf life.

Enjoy your homemade dried apricots as a snack, in trail mix, or use them in baking recipes.

Oatmeal Raisin Cookies

Ingredients:

1 cup unsalted butter, softened
1 cup granulated sugar
1 cup brown sugar
2 large eggs
1 teaspoon vanilla extract
2 cups all-purpose flour
1 teaspoon baking soda
1 teaspoon ground cinnamon
1/2 teaspoon salt
3 cups rolled oats
1 cup raisins

Instructions:

1. Preheat oven to 350°F (180°C).
2. In a large bowl, cream together the butter, granulated sugar, and brown sugar until light and fluffy.
3. Add the eggs and vanilla extract and beat until well combined.
4. In a separate bowl, whisk together the flour, baking soda, cinnamon, and salt.
5. Add the dry ingredients to the butter mixture and mix until just combined.
6. Stir in the oats and raisins.
7. Drop spoonfuls of dough onto baking sheets lined with parchment paper.
8. Bake for 12-15 minutes or until golden brown.
9. Cool on the baking sheets for 5 minutes, then transfer to a wire rack to cool completely.

Date Energy Balls

Ingredients:

1 cup pitted dates
1 cup almonds
1/4 cup honey
1/4 cup unsweetened cocoa powder
1/4 cup unsweetened shredded coconut
1 teaspoon vanilla extract

Instructions:

1. Place the dates and almonds in a food processor and pulse until finely chopped.
2. Add the honey, cocoa powder, coconut, and vanilla extract and process until the mixture comes together and forms a ball.
3. Scoop the mixture into tablespoon-sized balls and roll between your hands to smooth.
4. Store in an airtight container in the refrigerator for up to 2 weeks.
5. Place the dates and almonds in a food processor and pulse until finely chopped.
6. Add the honey, cocoa powder, coconut, and vanilla extract and process until the mixture comes together and forms a ball.
7. Scoop the mixture into tablespoon-sized balls and roll between your hands to smooth.
8. Store in an airtight container in the refrigerator for up to 2 weeks.

Chocolate Prune Cake

PALLARES
SOLSONA

Apricot Jam

Ingredients:

1 pound apricots, pitted and chopped
1 cup granulated sugar
1/4 cup lemon juice
Pinch of salt

Instructions:

1. In a medium saucepan, combine the apricots, sugar, lemon juice, and salt.
2. Cook over medium heat, stirring occasionally, until the apricots break down and the mixture thickens, about 20-30min.
3. Remove from heat and let cool slightly.
4. Transfer the mixture to a blender and blend until smooth.
5. Pour the jam into jars and let cool completely before storing in the refrigerator for up to 2 weeks.

Date & Walnut Energy Balls

Instructions:

1. In a food processor, blend 1 cup pitted dates, 1/2 cup walnuts, 1/4 cup of almond butter, 1 tablespoon of honey, & a pinch of salt until a sticky dough forms.
2. Roll the dough into 1-inch balls & coat with shredded coconut or cocoa powder, if desired.
3. Chill in the refrigerator for at least 30 minutes before serving.

Chocolate Prune Cake

Ingredients:

1 cup pitted prunes, chopped
1 cup boiling water
1/2 cup unsweetened cocoa powder
1 teaspoon baking soda
1/2 teaspoon salt
1 1/2 cups all-purpose flour
1/2 cup unsalted butter, softened
1 cup granulated sugar
2 large eggs
1 teaspoon vanilla extract
1/2 cup buttermilk

Instructions:

1. Preheat oven to 350°F (175°C). Grease a 9-inch cake pan with cooking spray.
2. In a medium bowl, combine chopped prunes and boiling water. Let stand for 10 minutes.
3. In a separate bowl, sift together cocoa powder, baking soda, salt, and flour.
4. In a large mixing bowl, cream the butter and sugar until light and fluffy. Add the eggs, one at a time, beating well after each addition. Stir in the vanilla extract.
5. Add the flour mixture to the butter mixture in three parts, alternating with the buttermilk, beginning and ending with the flour mixture.
6. Fold in the soaked prunes and their liquid.
7. Pour the batter into the prepared cake pan & smooth the surface.
8. Bake for 40-45 minutes, or until a toothpick inserted in the center comes out clean.
9. Remove from the oven and let cool in the pan for 10 minutes.
10. Invert the cake onto a wire rack and cool completely.
11. Dust with powdered sugar or cocoa powder before serving. Enjoy!

Spiced Apple Chips

Instructions:

1. Preheat oven to 225°F (110°C) and line a baking sheet with parchment paper.
2. Cut 2 large apples into thin slices and remove the seeds.
3. In a small bowl, mix 1 tablespoon of honey with 1 teaspoon of cinnamon and 1/4 teaspoon of nutmeg.
4. Brush the apple slices with the honey mixture and place them on the prepared baking sheet.
5. Bake for 2-3 hours or until the apples are dry and crispy.
6. Store in an airtight container.

Candied Ginger & Pineapple

Instructions:

1. Cut 1/2 cup of dried pineapple into small pieces and chop 1/4 cup of candied ginger.
2. In a small saucepan, combine 1/2 cup of sugar and 1/2 cup of water and bring to a boil.
3. Add the pineapple and ginger to the saucepan and simmer for 10-15 minutes or until the liquid has reduced and thickened.
4. Spread the mixture on a parchment-lined baking sheet and let it cool completely.
5. Break the candied fruit into small pieces and store in an airtight container.

Fig & Goat Cheese Salad

Fig & Goat Cheese Salad

Ingredients:

4 cups mixed salad greens
4 fresh figs, quartered
2 ounces crumbled goat cheese
1/4 cup chopped walnuts
2 tbl balsamic vinegar
2 tbl olive oil
Salt and pepper to taste

Instructions:

1. In a large bowl, combine the salad greens, figs, goat cheese and walnuts.
2. In a small bowl, whisk together the balsamic vinegar & olive oil.
3. Drizzle the dressing over the salad and toss to combine.
4. Season with salt and pepper to taste.

Figs

Ingredients:

Fresh figs
Granulated sugar
Water

Instructions:

1. Preheat your oven to 140°F (60°C) or its lowest setting.
2. Wash and dry your figs. Remove any stems and slice off a thin piece of the bottom of each fig.
3. Cut a cross into the top of each fig.
4. In a medium saucepan, bring 2 cups of water and 1 cup of sugar to a boil over high heat.
5. Reduce heat to medium-low and stir until sugar is dissolved.
6. Add figs to the sugar syrup and simmer for 5 minutes.
7. Using a slotted spoon, remove figs from the syrup and place them on a baking sheet lined with parchment paper.
8. Place the baking sheet in the oven and leave the oven door slightly open to allow moisture to escape.
9. Dry the figs in the oven for 12 to 24 hours, depending on the size and ripeness of the figs, until they are dry and leathery.
10. Once dry, remove from the oven and allow the figs to cool.
11. Store the figs in an airtight container at room temperature for up to 6 months.

Baked Honey Prunes

Ingredients:

1 pound pitted dried prunes
1/2 cup honey
1/2 cup water

2 cinnamon sticks
1 lemon, sliced

Instructions:

1. Preheat the oven to 350°F.
2. In a large baking dish, combine the prunes, honey, water, cinnamon sticks, and lemon slices. Mix well.
3. Cover the dish with foil and bake for 20-25 minutes.
4. Remove the foil and bake for an additional 10-15 minutes, or until the prunes are tender and the liquid has thickened.
5. Let the prunes cool slightly before serving. They can be served warm or at room temperature.
6. This recipe can be adjusted to your taste preferences by adding more or less honey or cinnamon, or by substituting the lemon with orange or other citrus fruit. The baked honey prunes can be enjoyed as a snack, served over ice cream or yogurt, or used as a topping for oatmeal or granola.

Dried Cherry & Almond Granola

Instructions:

1. Preheat oven to 300°F (150°C) and line a baking sheet with parchment paper.
2. In a large bowl, mix 3 cups of old-fashioned rolled oats, 1 cup of chopped almonds, 1/2 cup of dried cherries, 1/4 cup of brown sugar and 1/2 teaspoon of cinnamon.
3. In a small saucepan, warm 1/3 cup of honey and 1/4 cup of coconut oil until melted and smooth.
4. Pour the honey mixture over the oat mixture and stir until everything is well-coated.
5. Spread the granola on the prepared baking sheet and bake for 25-30 minutes or until golden brown.
6. Let it cool completely before breaking it into clusters and storing in an airtight container.

The Call of South Africa
(Die Stem van Suid Afrika) verses 1&4

Ringing out from our blue heavens,
From our deep seas breaking round;
Over everlasting mountains,
Where the echoing crags resound;
From our plains where creaking wagons
Cut their trails into the earth,
Calls the spirit of our country,
Of the land that gave us birth.
At thy call we shall not falter,
Firm and steadfast we shall stand,
At thy will to live or perish,
O South Africa, dear land.

In thy power, Almighty, trusting,
Did our fathers build of old;
Strengthen then, O Lord, their children
To defend, to love, to hold –
That the heritage they gave us
For our children yet may be:
Bondsmen only to the Highest
And before the whole world free.
As our fathers trusted humbly,
Teach us, Lord to trust Thee still:
Guard our land and guide our people
In Thy way to do Thy will.

Baked Prunes

Notes

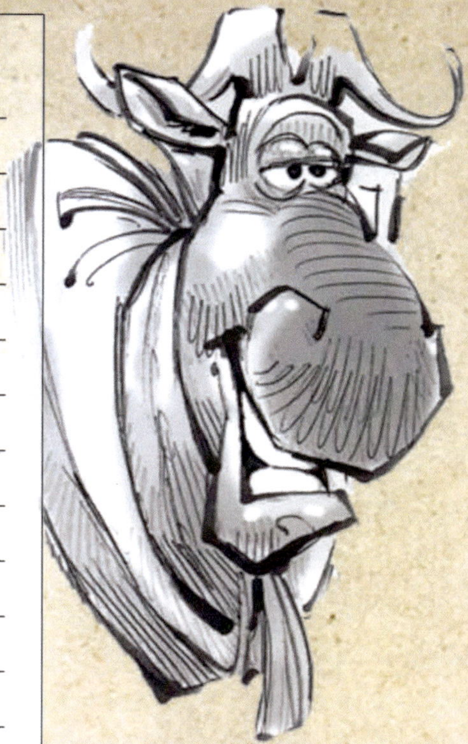

_____

_____

_____

_____

_____

_____

_____

_____

_____

_____

_____

_____

_____

_____

_____

_____

Notes

_____

_____

_____

_____

_____

_____

_____

_____

_____

_____

_____

_____

_____

_____

_____

_____

_____

Cape Malays

A little-known fact about South African history is the existence of a group called the "Cape Malays."

The Cape Malays are a distinct ethnic group in South Africa, primarily concentrated in the Western Cape region. They are descendants of enslaved people brought to the Cape Colony from various parts of Southeast Asia, including Malaysia, Indonesia, and India, during the 17th and 18th centuries.

These individuals were originally brought to the Cape Colony by the Dutch East India Company to work as laborers, servants, and skilled artisans. Over time, they developed their own unique culture, language (known as Cape Malay), and cuisine, which blended elements of their diverse ancestral backgrounds with local influences.

The Cape Malays played a significant role in shaping the cultural landscape of South Africa. Their contributions are particularly evident in the fields of music, cuisine, and architecture. For example, Cape Malay cuisine, characterized by its aromatic spices and flavors, is now considered an integral part of South African culinary heritage. The distinctive Cape Dutch architectural style, which combines elements of European and Asian design, is also attributed to the influence of the Cape Malays.

Despite their historical significance, the Cape Malays' contributions and experiences have often been overlooked or marginalized within broader narratives of South African history. However, their cultural heritage and identity continue to be celebrated by the local community and have gained recognition in recent years as an important part of the country's multicultural heritage.

Dadel Vingers

(DAH-duhl VING-ers)

Eight reasons why we love Dadel Vingers (Date Fingers)

Sweet and Chewy:
Dadel Vingers have a delightful chewy texture, thanks to the soft, gooey dates. The natural sweetness of the dates makes them a satisfying treat that appeals to the sweet tooth.

Crunchy Nuts:
Depending on the recipe variation, Dadel Vingers may contain chopped nuts like almonds, walnuts, or pecans. These nuts add a crunchy element to the soft and chewy dates, creating a pleasing contrast in texture.

Unique Flavors:
Dadel Vingers can be prepared with various flavor combinations, such as cinnamon, cardamom, orange zest, coconut, or almond extract. These unique flavors enhance the overall taste experience and make each bite exciting.

Finger Food:
The finger-like shape of Dadel Vingers adds a playful element to eating them. They can be picked up and enjoyed easily without the need for utensils, making them a fun snack to share or enjoy on the go.

Nostalgic Treat:
Dadel Vingers are often associated with cherished memories and family traditions, especially in South African communities. This nostalgic aspect adds to the enjoyment and comfort of eating them.

Perfect for Tea Time:
Dadel Vingers are a classic accompaniment to tea or coffee. They are often served during afternoon tea, making tea time feel extra special and enjoyable.

Versatility:
The different variations of Dadel Vingers offer versatility in taste and presentation. Each recipe can be tailored to personal preferences, allowing for creative experimentation and adaptation.

Cultural Connection:
For those with South African heritage or familiarity with Afrikaner cuisine, Dadel Vingers can evoke a sense of cultural connection and celebration.

Overall, Dadel Vingers offer a delightful combination of flavors, textures, and cultural significance, making them a joy to eat and share with loved ones.

Classic Dadel Vingers

Ingredients:

250g (1 1/4 cups) pitted dates, finely chopped
60g (1/2 cup) almonds, finely chopped *(walnuts/pecans)*
60ml (1/4 cup) water
5ml (1 tsp) vanilla extract
150g (1 1/4 cups) all-purpose flour
75g (1/3 cup) unsalted butter, softened
30ml (2 tbsp) honey or maple syrup
A pinch of salt

Instructions:

1. Preheat the oven to 180°C (350°F). Line a baking sheet with parchment paper.
2. In a bowl, combine the finely chopped dates, almonds (or other nuts), water, and vanilla extract. Mix well and set aside.
3. In a separate bowl, cream the softened butter and honey (or maple syrup) together until smooth.
4. Gradually add the flour and salt to the butter mixture, stirring until a soft dough forms.
5. Take small portions of the dough and roll them into finger-shaped logs.
6. Flatten each log slightly, then make a small indentation along the center.
7. Fill the indentation with the date and nut mixture.
8. Fold the dough over the filling, sealing it well, and roll it back into a finger shape.
9. Place the filled date fingers on the prepared baking sheet.
10. Bake in the preheated oven for 12-15 minutes, or until lightly golden.
11. Let the Dadel Vingers cool on a wire rack before serving.

Coconut & Lime Dadel Vingers

Ingredients:

250g (1 1/4 cups) pitted dates, finely chopped
60g (1/2 cup) chopped almonds *(walnuts/pecans for variation)*
60ml (1/4 cup) water
5ml (1 tsp) vanilla extract
30ml (2 tbsp) shredded coconut
Zest of 1 lime
150g (1 1/4 cups) all-purpose flour
75g (1/3 cup) unsalted butter, softened
30ml (2 tbsp) honey or maple syrup
A pinch of salt

Instructions:

1. Preheat oven to 180°C (350°F), Line a baking sheet with parchment paper.
2. In a bowl, combine the finely chopped dates, almonds (or other nuts), water, vanilla extract, shredded coconut, and lime zest. Mix well and set aside.
3. In a separate bowl, cream the softened butter and honey (or maple syrup) together until smooth.
4. Gradually add flour & salt to the butter mix, stir until a soft dough.
5. Take small portions dough and roll them into finger-shaped logs.
6. Flatten each log slightly, make a small indentation along the center.
7. Fill the indentation with the date and nut mixture.
8. Fold the dough over the filling, sealing it well, and roll it back into a finger shape.
9. Place the filled date fingers on the prepared baking sheet.
10. Bake in the preheated oven for 12-15min, or until lightly golden.
11. Let the Dadel Vingers cool on a wire rack before serving.

Orange & Ginger Dadel Vingers

Ingredients:

250g (1 1/4 cups) pitted dates, finely chopped
60g (1/2 cup) chopped almonds *(walnuts/pecans for variation)*
60ml (1/4 cup) water
5ml (1 tsp) vanilla extract
Zest of 1 orange
5ml (1 tsp) ground ginger
150g (1 1/4 cups) all-purpose flour
75g (1/3 cup) unsalted butter, softened
30ml (2 tbsp) honey or maple syrup
A pinch of salt

Instructions:

1. Preheat the oven to 180°C (350°F). Line a baking sheet with parchment paper.
2. In a bowl, combine the finely chopped dates, almonds (or other nuts), water, vanilla extract, orange zest, and ground ginger. Mix well and set aside.
3. In a separate bowl, cream the softened butter and honey (or maple syrup) together until smooth.
4. Gradually add the flour and salt to the butter mixture, stirring until a soft dough forms.
5. Take small portions of the dough and roll them into finger-shaped logs.
6. Flatten each log slightly, then make a small indentation along the center.
7. Fill the indentation with the date and nut mixture.
8. Fold the dough over the filling, sealing it well, and roll it back into a finger shape.
9. Place the filled date fingers on the prepared baking sheet.
10. Bake in the preheated oven for 12-15min, or until lightly golden.
11. Let the Dadel Vingers cool on a wire rack before serving.

Cinnamon & Cardamom Dadel Vingers

Ingredients:

250g (1 1/4 cups) pitted dates, finely chopped
60g (1/2 cup) chopped almonds *(walnuts/pecans or pistachios)*
60ml (1/4 cup) water
5ml (1 tsp) vanilla extract
5ml (1 tsp) ground cardamom
2.5ml (1/2 tsp) ground cinnamon
150g (1 1/4 cups) all-purpose flour
75g (1/3 cup) unsalted butter, softened
30ml (2 tbsp) honey or maple syrup
A pinch of salt

Instructions:

1. Preheat the oven to 180°C (350°F). Line a baking sheet with parchment paper.
2. In a bowl, combine the finely chopped dates, almonds (or other nuts), water, vanilla extract, ground cardamom, and ground cinnamon. Mix well and set aside.
3. In a separate bowl, cream the softened butter and honey (or maple syrup) together until smooth.
4. Gradually add the flour and salt to the butter mixture, stirring until a soft dough forms.
5. Take small portions dough and roll them into finger-shaped logs.
6. Flatten each log slightly, make a small indentation along the center.
7. Fill the indentation with the date and nut mixture.
8. Fold the dough over the filling, sealing it well, and roll it back into a finger shape.
9. Place the filled date fingers on the prepared baking sheet.
10. Bake in the preheated oven for 12-15min, or until lightly golden.
11. Let the Dadel Vingers cool on a wire rack before serving.

Notes

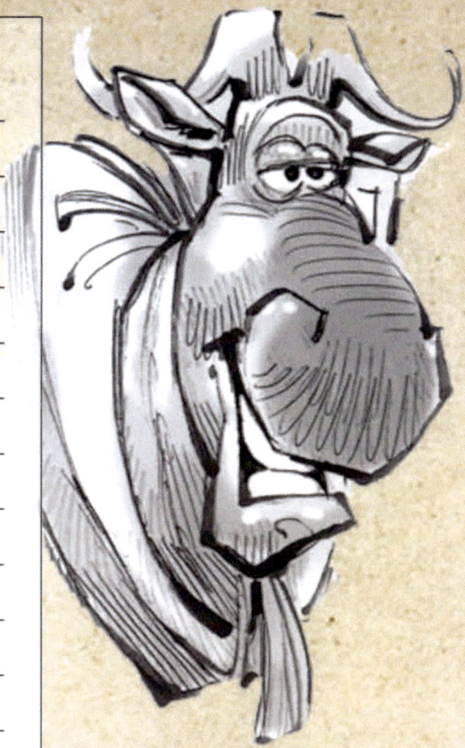

_____
_____
_____
_____
_____
_____
_____
_____
_____
_____
_____
_____
_____
_____
_____

Notes

_____
_____
_____
_____
_____
_____
_____
_____
_____
_____
_____
_____
_____
_____
_____
_____
_____
_____
_____

General Louis Botha

A Leader's Journey Towards South African Independence

General Louis Botha, born on September 27, 1862, in Greytown, Natal Province, embarked on an extraordinary journey that would shape the course of South African history and lead the nation toward independence. Botha's life was marked by his leadership during the Boer War, his contributions to the formation of the Union of South Africa, and his influential role as the country's first prime minister.

Early Life and Military Career

Louis Botha grew up in a farming family and demonstrated exceptional leadership qualities from an early age. He developed a deep connection to the land and its people, which would guide his actions throughout his life. After receiving a limited formal education, Botha became a successful farmer and gained prominence in the Zoutpansberg district.

When the Second Boer War broke out in 1899, Botha played a crucial role as a military leader. He led his commandos in numerous battles, demonstrating strategic brilliance and inspiring his fellow Boer fighters. His skills and determination earned him a reputation as a formidable opponent to British forces.

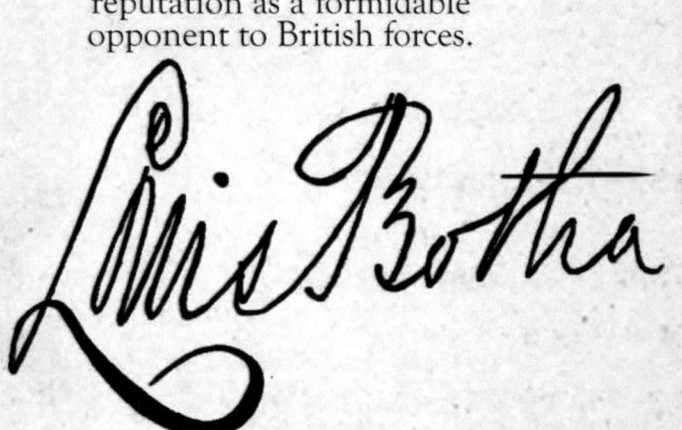

Negotiator and Statesman

After the Boer War, Botha recognized the need for peace and reconciliation. He emerged as a key negotiator during the peace talks that eventually led to the Treaty of Vereeniging in 1902, ending the war. Botha's commitment to finding a peaceful resolution and his willingness to work with former adversaries laid the foundation for his future political career.

Formation of the Union of South Africa

Botha's political aspirations gained momentum with the formation of the Union of South Africa in 1910. He played a pivotal role in uniting the former Boer republics and British colonies into a single nation. His leadership and diplomatic skills were crucial in navigating the complexities of uniting diverse regions and populations.

First Prime Minister of South Africa

In 1910, Botha became the first prime minister of the Union of South Africa. His tenure was marked by a focus on reconciliation and nation-building. Botha worked tirelessly to bridge the divides between Afrikaners and English-speaking South Africans, aiming to create a unified nation that could move beyond the scars of war.

Botha's leadership was also tested during World War I when South Africa entered the conflict as part of the British Empire. He faced internal divisions and resistance, but his steady leadership ensured that South Africa contributed effectively to the war effort.

Legacy and Impact

General Louis Botha's impact on South Africa's history cannot be overstated. He played a crucial role in transitioning the nation from war to peace, from colonial rule to independence. Botha's commitment to unite, reconciliation, and the well-being of his fellow South Africans shaped the foundations of a democratic and inclusive nation.

Botha's legacy as a leader and statesman endures, with his principles of cooperation and reconciliation continuing to influence South African politics. His commitment to the ideals of freedom, equality, and justice serves as an inspiration for future generations, reminding them of the power of leadership and the potential for positive change.

General Louis Botha's life stands as a testament to the resilience and determination of a visionary leader who played a pivotal role in shaping South Africa's destiny and laying the groundwork for a united and prosperous nation.

Louis Botha during the Boer War

Statue in Cape Town by Romano Romanelli

LOVIS BOTHA

FARMER

WARRIOR

STATESMAN

1862 - 1919

Melktert (Milk Tart)

The origins of Melktert, or Milk Tart, can be traced back to Dutch and Afrikaner culinary traditions in South Africa. It is believed to have its roots in the 17th century when Dutch settlers arrived in the Cape of Good Hope, bringing their culinary influences with them.

Melktert was likely inspired by various traditional Dutch desserts, such as custards and tarts. Over time, the Dutch settlers adapted their recipes to suit the ingredients available in the new region, incorporating local flavors and influences.

The early versions of Melktert were simple, featuring a pastry crust filled with milk, sugar, and eggs, often infused with cinnamon. As the dish gained popularity among the Dutch and Afrikaner communities, variations and regional differences in preparation and flavors emerged.

Melktert became a treasured part of South African culinary heritage, passed down through generations. Today, it remains a beloved dessert in South Africa, enjoyed on special occasions, holidays, and as a comforting treat to accompany a cup of tea or coffee.

The dish's popularity has also transcended South Africa's borders, and variations of Milk Tart can now be found in other countries with historical connections to Dutch and Afrikaner cultures.

While the exact origin of Melktert may be challenging to pinpoint, its enduring popularity and cultural significance in South Africa make it a cherished dessert that continues to be savored and celebrated by people of diverse backgrounds.

Handy Tips

Pastry Crust:
For a delicious Melktert, ensure that the pastry crust is well-baked and crisp. Blind baking the crust before adding the filling can help prevent a soggy bottom. You can use pie weights or dry beans on parchment paper to weigh down the crust during blind baking.

Custard Filling:
When making the custard filling, stir it constantly over low to medium heat to avoid lumps and ensure a smooth texture. Be patient and don't rush the process. Properly thickened custard will set nicely and give the Melktert a creamy consistency.

Flavorings:
While traditional Melktert is flavored with cinnamon, you can experiment with other flavorings such as lemon zest, almond extract, or even a hint of nutmeg to add unique twists to the dessert.

Remember, baking is a creative process, and making Melktert can be a delightful culinary adventure.
Don't be afraid to experiment and make it your own. Enjoy the process and savor the delicious results!

Cooling & Setting

After baking:
Allow the Melktert to cool completely before slicing and serving. This will help the custard set properly and make it easier to cut into clean slices.

Serving:
Melktert is traditionally served chilled or at room temperature. Before serving, you can dust the top with cinnamon, cocoa powder, or nutmeg for an attractive finish.

Storing:
If you have leftovers, store them in the refrigerator in an airtight container to maintain freshness. Melktert can be enjoyed for a few days, but it's best when consumed within 2-3 days of making.

Variations:
Feel free to get creative and try different variations of Melktert. You can experiment with different types of crusts, fillings (like chocolate or coffee-flavored custard), or even try making mini tarts for individual servings.

Consistency:
If you find that the custard is too runny, you can add a little more cornstarch to the filling mixture next time. On the other hand, if the custard is too thick, you can use slightly less cornstarch.

Whipped Cream:
To add a delightful touch, you can serve Melktert with a dollop of freshly whipped cream /a sprinkling of ground cinnamon /cocoa powder on top.

Classic Melktert

Ingredients:

For the crust:
200g (1 2/3 cups) all-purpose flour
100g (7 tablespoons) unsalted butter, cold and cubed
50g (1/4 cup) granulated sugar
1 large egg, beaten

For the filling:
750ml (3 cups) whole milk
2 tablespoons (30ml) unsalted butter
2 large eggs
100g (1/2 cup) granulated sugar
50g (1/4 cup) all-purpose flour
50g (1/4 cup) cornstarch
1 teaspoon vanilla extract
A pinch of salt
Ground cinnamon or nutmeg, for dusting

Instructions:

Crust Instructions:
1. Preheat your oven to 180°C (350°F).
2. In a bowl, mix the flour and sugar. Add the cold cubed butter and rub it into the flour mixture until it resembles breadcrumbs.
3. Add the beaten egg and knead until you have a smooth dough.
4. Wrap the dough in plastic wrap and refrigerate for 30 minutes.
5. Roll out the chilled dough on a floured surface and line a greased 9-inch tart pan (or 23cm) with the pastry.
6. Trim any excess dough.

Filling Instructions:
1. In a saucepan, heat the milk and butter until it's just about to boil.
2. In a separate bowl, whisk together the eggs, sugar, flour, cornstarch, vanilla extract, and salt until well combined.
3. Slowly pour the hot milk mixture into the egg mixture, whisking continuously to avoid curdling.
4. Pour the combined mixture back into the saucepan.
5. Cook the filling over low to medium heat, stirring constantly until it thickens and reaches a custard-like consistency.
6. Pour the hot filling into the prepared crust.
7. Bake the Melktert in the preheated oven for about 25-30 minutes or until the filling is set and the crust is golden.
8. Allow the Melktert to cool completely in the pan before dusting the top with ground cinnamon or nutmeg.
9. Once cooled, remove the tart from the pan and serve chilled.

Chocolate Melktert

Ingredients:

For the crust:
180g (1 1/2 cups) all-purpose flour
90g (6 tablespoons) unsalted butter, cold and cubed
40g (3 tablespoons) granulated sugar
2 tablespoons (30g) cocoa powder
1 large egg, beaten

For the filling:
750ml (3 cups) whole milk
2 tablespoons (30ml) unsalted butter
2 large eggs
100g (1/2 cup) granulated sugar
50g (1/4 cup) all-purpose flour
50g (1/4 cup) cornstarch
2 tablespoons (30g) cocoa powder
1 teaspoon vanilla extract
A pinch of salt
Chocolate shavings or cocoa powder, for dusting

Instructions:

Crust Instructions:
1. Preheat your oven to 180°C (350°F).
2. In a bowl, mix the flour and sugar. Add the cold cubed butter and rub it into the flour mixture until it resembles breadcrumbs.
3. Add the beaten egg and knead until you have a smooth dough.
4. Wrap the dough in plastic wrap and refrigerate for 30 minutes.
5. Roll out the chilled dough on a floured surface and line a greased 9-inch tart pan (or 23cm) with the pastry.
6. Trim any excess dough.

Filling Instructions:
1. In a saucepan, heat the milk and butter until it's just about to boil.
2. In a separate bowl, whisk together the eggs, sugar, flour, cornstarch, cocoa powder, vanilla extract & salt until well combined.
3. Slowly pour the hot milk mixture into the egg mixture, whisking continuously to avoid curdling.
4. Pour the combined mixture back into the saucepan.
5. Cook the filling over low to medium heat, stirring constantly until it thickens and reaches a custard-like consistency.
6. Pour the hot filling into the prepared crust.
7. Bake the Chocolate Milk Tart in the preheated oven for about 25-30 minutes or until the filling is set and the crust is golden.
8. Allow the tart to cool completely before garnishing with chocolate shavings or cocoa powder.

Lemon Melktert

Ingredients:

For the crust:
200g (1 2/3 cups) all-purpose flour
100g (7 tbls) unsalted butter, cold & cubed
50g (1/4 cup) granulated sugar
Zest of 1 lemon
1 large egg, beaten

For the filling:
750ml (3 cups) whole milk
2 tablespoons (30ml) unsalted butter
2 large eggs
100g (1/2 cup) granulated sugar
50g (1/4 cup) all-purpose flour
50g (1/4 cup) cornstarch
Zest of 2 lemons
1 teaspoon vanilla extract
A pinch of salt
Powdered sugar and lemon zest, for garnish

Crust Instructions:
1. Preheat your oven to 180°C (350°F).
2. In a bowl, mix the flour and sugar. Add the cold cubed butter and rub it into the flour mixture until it resembles breadcrumbs.
3. Add the beaten egg and knead until you have a smooth dough.
4. Wrap the dough in plastic wrap and refrigerate for 30 minutes.
5. Roll out the chilled dough on a floured surface and line a greased 9-inch tart pan (or 23cm) with the pastry.
6. Trim any excess dough.

Filling Instructions:
1. In a saucepan, heat the milk and butter until it's just about to boil.
2. In a separate bowl, whisk together the eggs, sugar, flour, cornstarch, lemon zest, vanilla extract, and salt until well combined.
3. Slowly pour the hot milk mixture into the egg mixture, whisking continuously to avoid curdling.
4. Pour the combined mixture back into the saucepan.
5. Cook the filling over low to medium heat, stirring constantly until it thickens and reaches a custard-like consistency.
6. Pour the hot filling into the prepared crust.
7. Bake the Lemon Milk Tart in the preheated oven for about 25-30 minutes or until the filling is set and the crust is golden.
8. Allow the tart to cool completely before garnishing with powdered sugar and additional lemon zest.

Cremora Tart
Coffee Cream Pie

Ingredients:

250 grams Cremora / Powdered Coffee Creamer
125 ml Cold Water
125 ml Lemon juice
1 tin Condensed milk
1 packet Tennis biscuits

Instructions:

Use Electric Mixer

1. Mix the cremora/coffee creamer and cold water until smooth
2. Add the condensed milk and mix well
3. Add the lemon juice and mix until the mixture thickens
4. Pour over the tennis biscuits and allow to set in the fridge for about 10 minutes

Coconut Melktert

Ingredients:

For the crust:
180g (1 1/2 cups) all-purpose flour
90g (6 tablespoons) unsalted butter, cold and cubed
40g (3 tablespoons) granulated sugar
30g (1/4 cup) desiccated coconut
1 large egg, beaten

For the filling:
750ml (3 cups) coconut milk
2 tablespoons (30ml) coconut oil
2 large eggs
100g (1/2 cup) granulated sugar
50g (1/4 cup) all-purpose flour
50g (1/4 cup) cornstarch
1 teaspoon vanilla extract
A pinch of salt
Toasted coconut flakes, for garnish

Instructions:

Crust Instructions:
1. Preheat your oven to 180°C (350°F).
2. In a bowl, mix the flour and sugar. Add the cold cubed butter and rub it into the flour mixture until it resembles breadcrumbs.
3. Add the beaten egg and knead until you have a smooth dough.
4. Wrap the dough in plastic wrap and refrigerate for 30 minutes.
5. Roll out the chilled dough on a floured surface and line a greased 9-inch tart pan (or 23cm) with the pastry.
6. Trim any excess dough.

Filling Instructions:
1. In a saucepan, heat the coconut milk and coconut oil until it's just about to boil.
2. In a separate bowl, whisk together the eggs, sugar, flour, cornstarch, vanilla extract, and salt until well combined.
3. Slowly pour the hot coconut milk mixture into the egg mixture, whisking continuously to avoid curdling.
4. Pour the combined mixture back into the saucepan.
5. Cook the filling over low to medium heat, stirring constantly until it thickens and reaches a custard-like consistency.
6. Pour the hot filling into the prepared crust.
7. Bake the Coconut Milk Tart in the preheated oven for about 25-30 minutes or until the filling is set and the crust is golden.
8. Allow the tart to cool completely before garnishing with toasted coconut flakes.

Coffee Melktert

Ingredients:

For the crust:
200g (1 2/3 cups) all-purpose flour
100g (7 tablespoons) unsalted butter, cold and cubed
50g (1/4 cup) granulated sugar
2 tablespoons instant coffee powder
1 large egg, beaten

For the filling:
750ml (3 cups) whole milk
2 tablespoons (30ml) unsalted butter
2 large eggs
100g (1/2 cup) granulated sugar
50g (1/4 cup) all-purpose flour
50g (1/4 cup) cornstarch
2 tablespoons instant coffee powder
1 teaspoon vanilla extract
A pinch of salt
Whipped cream and chocolate shavings, for garnish

Instructions:

Crust Instructions:
1. Preheat your oven to 180°C (350°F).
2. In a bowl, mix the flour and sugar. Add the cold cubed butter and rub it into the flour mixture until it resembles breadcrumbs.
3. Add the beaten egg and knead until you have a smooth dough.
4. Wrap the dough in plastic wrap and refrigerate for 30 minutes.
5. Roll out the chilled dough on a floured surface and line a greased 9-inch tart pan (or 23cm) with the pastry.
6. Trim any excess dough.

Filling Instructions:
1. In a saucepan, heat the milk and butter until it's just about to boil. Dissolve the instant coffee powder in the milk mixture.
2. In a separate bowl, whisk together the eggs, sugar, flour, cornstarch, instant coffee powder, vanilla extract, and salt until well combined.
3. Slowly pour the hot milk mixture into the egg mixture, whisking continuously to avoid curdling.
4. Pour the combined mixture back into the saucepan.
5. Cook the filling over low to medium heat, stirring constantly until it thickens and reaches a custard-like consistency.
6. Pour the hot filling into the prepared crust.
7. Bake the Coffee Milk Tart in the preheated oven for about 25-30min or until the filling is set and the crust is golden.
8. Allow the tart to cool completely before garnishing with whipped cream and chocolate shavings.

Notes

Notes

Pannekoek (Pancakes)

Pannekoek, pronounced as "pan-uh-kook," is a traditional South African pancake known for its thin, large, and slightly sweet texture. It is a popular and can be enjoyed with a variety of toppings. Pannekoek is commonly found in South African restaurants, tearooms, and family homes, where it is served with various toppings and fillings, both sweet and savory.

Classic Pannekoek

Ingredients:

200g (1 1/2 cups) all-purpose flour
15ml (1 tbsp) granulated sugar
A pinch of salt
500ml (2 cups) milk
3 large eggs
30ml (2 tbsp) melted butter
Additional butter for frying

Instructions:

1. In a mixing bowl, whisk together the flour, sugar, and salt.
2. In a separate bowl, beat the eggs and then add the milk and melted butter. Mix well.
3. Gradually add the wet ingredients to the dry ingredients, stirring until a smooth batter forms.
4. Heat a non-stick frying pan over medium heat and add a small amount of butter to coat the surface.
5. Pour about 60ml (1/4 cup) of the batter into the pan, swirling it around to evenly coat the bottom.
6. Cook the pancake for about 2 minutes on each side until golden brown.
7. Repeat the process with the remaining batter, adding more butter to the pan as needed.
8. Serve the Pannekoek warm with your favorite toppings such as powdered sugar, fruit, syrup, or jam.

Cheese & Ham Pannekoek

Ingredients:

200g (1 1/2 cups) all-purpose flour
5ml (1 tsp) baking powder
A pinch of salt
500ml (2 cups) milk
3 large eggs
30ml (2 tbsp) melted butter
100g (1 cup) shredded Gouda cheese
100g (1 cup) cooked ham, diced
Additional butter for frying

Instructions:

1. In a mixing bowl, whisk together the flour, baking powder, & salt.
2. In a separate bowl, beat the eggs and then add the milk and melted butter. Mix well.
3. Gradually add the wet ingredients to the dry ingredients, stirring until a smooth batter forms.
4. Stir in the shredded Gouda cheese and diced ham.
5. Heat a non-stick frying pan over medium heat and add a small amount of butter to coat the surface.
6. Pour about 60ml (1/4 cup) of the batter into the pan, swirling it around to evenly coat the bottom.
7. Cook the pancake for about 2 minutes on each side until golden brown and the cheese is melted.
8. Repeat the process with the remaining batter, adding more butter to the pan as needed.
9. Serve the Cheese and Ham Pannekoek warm with a dollop of sour cream and fresh chives.

"Did somebody say Pancakes?"

(Enjoy these delicious and versatile Pannekoek recipes for breakfast, brunch, or any time you crave a delightful treat!)

Apple Cinnamon Pannekoek

Ingredients:

200g (1 1/2 cups) all-purpose flour
5ml (1 tsp) baking powder
5ml (1 tsp) ground cinnamon
A pinch of salt
500ml (2 cups) milk
3 large eggs
30ml (2 tbsp) melted butter
2 medium apples, thinly sliced
30ml (2 tbsp) brown sugar
Additional butter for frying

Instructions:

1. In a mixing bowl, whisk together the flour, baking powder, ground cinnamon, and salt.
2. In a separate bowl, beat the eggs and then add the milk and melted butter. Mix well.
3. Gradually add the wet ingredients to the dry ingredients, stirring until a smooth batter forms.
4. In a separate bowl, toss the thinly sliced apples with brown sugar.
5. Heat a non-stick frying pan over medium heat and add a small amount of butter to coat the surface.
6. Pour about 60ml (1/4 cup) of the batter into the pan, swirling it around to evenly coat the bottom.
7. Arrange some apple slices on top of the pancake and press them gently into the batter.
8. Cook the pancake for about 2 minutes on each side until golden brown and the apples are tender.
9. Repeat the process with the remaining batter and apple slices, adding more butter to the pan as needed.
10. Serve the Apple Cinnamon Pannekoek warm with a drizzle of honey or maple syrup.

Nutella & Banana Pannekoek

Ingredients:

200g (1 1/2 cups) all-purpose flour
5ml (1 tsp) baking powder
A pinch of salt
500ml (2 cups) milk
3 large eggs
30ml (2 tbsp) melted butter
100g (1/2 cup) Nutella spread
2 ripe bananas, sliced
Additional butter for frying

Instructions:

1. In a mixing bowl, whisk together the flour, baking powder, and salt.
2. In a separate bowl, beat the eggs and then add the milk and melted butter. Mix well.
3. Gradually add the wet ingredients to the dry ingredients, stirring until a smooth batter forms.
4. Heat a non-stick frying pan over medium heat and add a small amount of butter to coat the surface.
5. Pour about 60ml (1/4 cup) of the batter into the pan, swirling it around to evenly coat the bottom.
6. Drop small spoonfuls of Nutella onto the pancake and swirl it around with a toothpick or knife.
7. Arrange banana slices on top of the pancake.
8. Cook the pancake for about 2 minutes on each side until golden brown and the Nutella is slightly melted.
9. Repeat the process with the remaining batter and banana slices, adding more butter to the pan as needed.
10. Serve the Nutella and Banana Pannekoek warm with a dusting of powdered sugar.

Savory Spinach & Feta Pannekoek

Ingredients:

200g (1 1/2 cups) all-purpose flour
5ml (1 tsp) baking powder
A pinch of salt
500ml (2 cups) milk
3 large eggs
30ml (2 tbsp) melted butter
100g (1 cup) fresh spinach, chopped
100g (1/2 cup) crumbled feta cheese
Additional butter for frying

Instructions:

1. In a mixing bowl, whisk together the flour, baking powder, and salt.
2. In a separate bowl, beat the eggs and then add the milk and melted butter. Mix well.
3. Gradually add the wet ingredients to the dry ingredients, stirring until a smooth batter forms.
4. Stir in the chopped fresh spinach and crumbled feta cheese.
5. Heat a non-stick frying pan over medium heat and add a small amount of butter to coat the surface.
6. Pour 60ml (1/4 cup) of the batter into the pan, swirling it around to evenly coat the bottom.
7. Cook pancake for about 2min on each side until golden brown & the feta is slightly melted.
8. Repeat the process with the remaining batter, adding more butter to the pan as needed.
9. Serve the Savory Spinach and Feta Pannekoek warm with a dollop of Greek yogurt and a sprinkle of black pepper.

Notes

Notes

General Jan Smuts

The Remarkable Life of a Statesman, Soldier, and Environmentalist

In the vast and diverse land of South Africa, a remarkable man named Jan Smuts lived a life that left an indelible mark on the nation's history. Born on May 24, 1870, in the rugged and beautiful Cape Colony, Jan Christiaan Smuts became a prominent statesman, soldier, and philosopher.

As a young boy, Jan Smuts developed a deep love for nature, spending countless hours exploring the untamed wilderness and finding solace in its serenity. This connection with the natural world profoundly influenced his thinking and perspective on life.

Driven by a thirst for knowledge, Jan Smuts pursued his education at Victoria College (now the University of Stellenbosch) and later at the University of Cambridge in England. His brilliance and intellectual curiosity led him to study law and delve into philosophy, science, and history.

Jan Smuts was not only a scholar but also a man of action. During the war between the British Empire and the Boer Republics, he fought with great courage on the side of the Boers, earning respect even from his adversaries despite their eventual defeat.

In the years that followed, Jan Smuts became a prominent figure in the British government, working alongside renowned leaders such as Winston Churchill. He played a vital role in the formation of the Union of South Africa, advocating for the inclusion of all South Africans, regardless of race or background.

Devoted to justice and equality, Smuts championed the idea of a multi-racial democracy and played a crucial role in drafting the South African Constitution to protect the rights of all citizens.

Beyond politics, Jan Smuts was a visionary environmentalist. He established national parks and worked towards preserving South Africa's unique flora and fauna, recognizing the importance of protecting the natural world for the well-being of humanity.

Throughout his life, Jan Smuts faced challenges but remained committed to a better South Africa—a nation of harmony, thriving nature, justice, and equality.

Jan Smuts passed away on September 11, 1950, leaving behind a lasting legacy that continues to inspire. His contributions to South Africa's history are a testament to intellect, compassion, and perseverance.

And so, as we turn the pages of history (and this recipe book), remember Jan Smuts—a man whose profound understanding of the world, dedication to his ideals, and love for his country made a significant difference in shaping the course of a nation. May his story inspire generations to come, reminding us that one person can indeed make a lasting impact on a nation's journey.

Statue of Jan Smuts, Parliament Square

Large cast medal 1947 made in The Netherlands, designed by G. Brinkgreve. Only a few of these medals were struck of which one was presented to Gen. Smuts.

Koeksister

A Koeksister (also spelled "koeksuster") is a traditional South African sweet treat that originated from the Afrikaner culinary heritage. It is a syrup-drenched, plaited pastry made from a twisted, braided dough that is deep-fried until golden and crispy.

The dough for Koeksisters is typically flavored with spices such as cinnamon, ginger, or nutmeg, giving them a fragrant and delicious taste. Once the pastry is fried to perfection, it is immediately dipped in a cold sugar syrup while still hot, allowing the syrup to soak into the pastry and sweeten it.

The result is a delectable, sticky, and syrupy confection with a crunchy exterior and a soft, sweet interior. Koeksisters are often served as a dessert or snack, and they are enjoyed throughout South Africa and in other parts of the world with South African communities.

Due to the unique combination of textures and flavors, Koeksisters have become a beloved treat and are an essential part of South Africa's culinary heritage. They are best enjoyed fresh and are a delightful indulgence for anyone with a sweet tooth.

The Koeksister Monument in Orania

(The Koeksister monument in Orania was erected as a tribute to those women who over decades baked koeksisters to raise money at bazaars for churches, schools, children's and old people's homes. This memorial was erected by Orania's Barefoot Women's Association and unveiled in September 2003 by Anna Boshoff, the daughter of Dr. H.F. Verwoerd. It is 2 m high and consists of polystyrene covered with fiberglass. Jan-Otto du Plessis from Cape Town was the sculptor.)

Koeksister Recipe

Delicious Koeksister Recipe:
Traditional South African Sweet Treat

Ingredients:

500g (4 cups) all-purpose flour
10g (2 tsp) ground cinnamon
10g (2 tsp) baking powder
1g (1/4 tsp) salt
60g (1/4 cup) unsalted butter, melted
250ml (1 cup) milk
1 large egg
Oil, for deep-frying

For the Syrup:
500g (2 1/2 cups) granulated sugar
250ml (1 cup) water
5ml (1 tsp) vanilla extract
5ml (1 tsp) lemon juice

Instructions:

1. In a large mixing bowl, sift together the flour, ground cinnamon, baking powder, and salt. Add the melted butter, milk, and egg to form a soft dough. Knead the dough until smooth and well combined.
2. Cover the dough with a damp cloth and let it rest for 30 minutes.
3. In the meantime, prepare the syrup by combining the granulated sugar, water, vanilla extract, and lemon juice in a saucepan. Bring the mixture to a boil, stirring until the sugar dissolves. Simmer the syrup for 5 minutes, then remove it from heat and let it cool.
4. After the dough has rested, roll it out on a floured surface to a thickness of about 1 cm (0.4 inches). Cut the dough into strips about 1.5 cm (0.6 inches) wide and 10 cm (4 inches) long.
5. Take each strip of dough and make a lengthwise slit in the center, leaving the top and bottom edges intact. Pull one end of the strip through the slit to create a twist or braid-like shape. Repeat with the remaining strips of dough.
6. Heat the oil in a deep-fryer or large pot to 180°C (350°F). Fry the Koeksisters in batches until they are golden brown and crispy, about 2-3 minutes per batch. Remove them from the oil using a slotted spoon and drain on a paper towel.
7. While the Koeksisters are still hot, immerse them in the cooled syrup, ensuring they are fully coated. Allow them to soak in the syrup for a few minutes.
8. Once soaked, remove the Koeksisters from the syrup and place them on a wire rack to cool completely.
9. Serve the Koeksisters at room temperature and enjoy this delicious South African treat!

Remember, Koeksisters are a versatile treat, and you can get creative with various flavor combinations to suit your taste preferences. Whether you're adding fruits, nuts, spices, or extracts, these variations will add a delightful twist to the traditional Koeksister recipe and make them even more enjoyable!

Storage:
Koeksisters are best enjoyed fresh but can be stored in an airtight container at room temperature for up to 2 days. For longer storage, freeze them in airtight containers for up to 2 months. To reheat, let them come to room temperature and enjoy!

Variations:
To add variations to the Koeksister recipe and create unique flavors, you can experiment with different ingredients and flavorings.

Here are some ideas to get you started:

Coconut Flavored Koeksisters:
Add 50g (1/2 cup) desiccated coconut to the dough mixture for a delightful coconut twist. Optionally, you can also infuse the syrup with coconut flavor by adding 5ml (1 tsp) of coconut extract.

Lemon or Orange Zest Koeksisters:
Add the zest of 1 lemon or orange to the dough mixture for a refreshing citrus flavor. You can also add a small amount (2.5ml or 1/2 tsp) of lemon or orange extract to enhance the flavor.

Spiced Koeksisters:
Add 5g (1 tsp) of mixed spice (a blend of cinnamon, nutmeg, and allspice) to the dough mixture for a warm and aromatic taste.

Raisin or Sultana Koeksisters:
Mix in 100g (3/4 cup) of raisins or sultanas to the dough for added sweetness and texture.

Almond or Pecan Koeksisters:
Mix in 100g (3/4 cup) of chopped almonds or pecans to the dough for a nutty flavor and crunch.

Chocolate Coated with Sprinkles:
After soaking the Koeksisters in the syrup, dip them in melted chocolate and sprinkle with colorful sprinkles for a festive treat.

Coffee or Cocoa Flavored Koeksisters:
Add 15ml (1 tbsp) of instant coffee or cocoa powder to the dough mixture for a subtle coffee or chocolate twist.

Rosewater or Orange Blossom Water:
Substitute 5ml (1 tsp) of vanilla extract in the syrup with rosewater or orange blossom water for a fragrant and exotic taste.

Notes

Notes

Pieter Mauritz Retief

(12 Nov 1780 – 6 Feb 1838)
was a Voortrekker leader.

He became a spokesperson
for the frontier farmers
who voiced their
discontent, and wrote
the Voortrekkers'
declaration at their
departure from the
colony.

He was a leading
figure during their
Great Trek, and at
one stage their
elected governor.

*Granite statue of Piet Retief,
Governor of the Voortrekkers,
at the north eastern corner of
the Voortrekker Monument,
Pretoria.*

Malva Pudding

Malva Pudding is a classic South African dessert known for its rich, sticky, and indulgent taste. It is a moist sponge cake drenched in a sweet and buttery sauce, making it a delightful treat loved by many.

Classic Malva Pudding

Ingredients:

250g (1 1/4 cups) granulated sugar
2 large eggs
15ml (1 tbsp) smooth apricot jam
200g (1 2/3 cups) all-purpose flour
5ml (1 tsp) baking soda (bicarbonate of soda)
A pinch of salt
250ml (1 cup) milk
15ml (1 tbsp) vinegar
30ml (2 tbsp) melted butter
For the Sauce:
250ml (1 cup) heavy cream
125g (1/2 cup) unsalted butter
125ml (1/2 cup) granulated sugar
125ml (1/2 cup) hot water

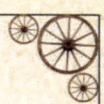

Instructions:

1. Preheat your oven to 180°C (350°F) and grease a baking dish (approximately 20x20cm or 8x8 inches).
2. In a large mixing bowl, cream together the sugar and eggs until light and fluffy.
3. Add the apricot jam to the egg mixture and beat until well combined.
4. In a separate bowl, sift the flour, baking soda, and salt together.
5. Mix the milk and vinegar in a measuring jug and let it sit for a few minutes to create a buttermilk substitute.
6. Gradually add the dry ingredients and the buttermilk mixture to the egg mixture, alternating between the two, and mixing until a smooth batter forms.
7. Stir in the melted butter.
8. Pour the batter into the prepared baking dish and smooth the top.
9. Bake the pudding in the preheated oven for about 30-40 min or until it is golden and a toothpick inserted into the center comes out clean.
10. While the pudding is baking, prepare the sauce. In a saucepan, combine the heavy cream, unsalted butter, granulated sugar, and hot water. Heat the mixture over low heat until the butter has melted and the sugar has dissolved. Do not boil.
11. When the pudding is done baking, remove it from the oven and immediately pour the hot sauce over the hot pudding.
12. Allow the pudding to absorb the sauce for a few minutes before serving.
13. Serve the Malva Pudding warm with a scoop of vanilla ice cream or a dollop of whipped cream.

Chocolate Malva Pudding

Ingredients:

250g (1 1/4 cups) granulated sugar
2 large eggs
15ml (1 tbsp) smooth apricot jam
200g (1 2/3 cups) all-purpose flour
5ml (1 tsp) baking soda (bicarbonate of soda)
A pinch of salt
30g (1/4 cup) cocoa powder
250ml (1 cup) milk
15ml (1 tbsp) vinegar
30ml (2 tbsp) melted butter

For the Chocolate Sauce:
250ml (1 cup) heavy cream
125g (1/2 cup) unsalted butter
125ml (1/2 cup) granulated sugar
60ml (1/4 cup) hot water
30g (1/4 cup) cocoa powder

Instructions:

1. Preheat your oven to 180°C (350°F) and grease a baking dish (approximately 20x20cm or 8x8 inches).
2. In a large mixing bowl, cream together the sugar and eggs until light and fluffy.
3. Add the apricot jam to the egg mixture and beat until well combined.
4. In a separate bowl, sift the flour, baking soda, & salt together.
5. Mix the milk and vinegar in a measuring jug and let it sit for a few minutes to create a buttermilk substitute.
6. Gradually add the dry ingredients and the buttermilk mixture to the egg mixture, alternating between the two, and mixing until a smooth batter forms.
7. Stir in the melted butter.
8. Pour the batter into the prepared baking dish and smooth the top.
9. In a separate saucepan, combine the heavy cream, unsalted butter, granulated sugar, hot water, and cocoa powder for the chocolate sauce. Heat the mixture over low heat until the butter has melted and the sugar has dissolved. Do not boil.
10. When the pudding is done baking, remove it from the oven and immediately pour the hot chocolate sauce over the hot pudding.
11. Allow the pudding to absorb the sauce for a few minutes before serving.
12. Serve the Chocolate Malva Pudding warm with a scoop of vanilla ice cream or a drizzle of chocolate syrup.

Coconut Malva Pudding

Ingredients:

250g (1 1/4 cups) granulated sugar
2 large eggs
15ml (1 tbsp) smooth apricot jam
200g (1 2/3 cups) all-purpose flour
5ml (1 tsp) baking soda (bicarbonate of soda)
A pinch of salt
125ml (1/2 cup) desiccated coconut
250ml (1 cup) coconut milk
15ml (1 tbsp) vinegar
30ml (2 tbsp) melted butter

For the Coconut Sauce:
250ml (1 cup) coconut cream
125g (1/2 cup) unsalted butter
125ml (1/2 cup) granulated sugar
125ml (1/2 cup) hot water

Instructions:

1. Preheat your oven to 180°C (350°F) and grease a baking dish (approximately 20x20cm or 8x8 inches).
2. In a large mixing bowl, cream together the sugar and eggs until light and fluffy.
3. Add the apricot jam to the egg mixture and beat until well combined.
4. In a separate bowl, sift the flour, baking soda, and salt together.
5. Mix the milk and vinegar in a measuring jug and let it sit for a few minutes to create a buttermilk substitute.
6. Gradually add the dry ingredients and the buttermilk mixture to the egg mixture, alternating between the two, and mixing until a smooth batter forms.
7. Stir in the melted butter.
8. Pour the batter into the prepared baking dish and smooth the top.
9. Mix the desiccated coconut into the batter before pouring it into the baking dish.
10. For the coconut sauce, combine the coconut cream, unsalted butter, granulated sugar, and hot water in a saucepan. Heat the mixture over low heat until the butter has melted and the sugar has dissolved. Do not boil.
11. When the pudding is done baking, remove it from the oven and immediately pour the hot coconut sauce over the hot pudding.
12. Allow the pudding to absorb the sauce for a few minutes before serving.
13. Serve the Coconut Malva Pudding warm with a sprinkle of toasted coconut on top.

Orange Malva Pudding

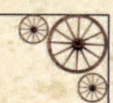

Ingredients:

250g (1 1/4 cups) granulated sugar
2 large eggs
15ml (1 tbsp) smooth apricot jam
200g (1 2/3 cups) all-purpose flour
5ml (1 tsp) baking soda (bicarbonate of soda)
A pinch of salt
Zest of 1 orange
250ml (1 cup) milk
15ml (1 tbsp) vinegar
30ml (2 tbsp) melted butter

For the Orange Sauce:
250ml (1 cup) fresh orange juice
125g (1/2 cup) unsalted butter
125ml (1/2 cup) granulated sugar

Instructions:

1. Preheat your oven to 180°C (350°F) and grease a baking dish (approximately 20x20cm or 8x8 inches).
2. In a large mixing bowl, cream together the sugar and eggs until light and fluffy.
3. Add the apricot jam to the egg mixture and beat until well combined.
4. In a separate bowl, sift the flour, baking soda, and salt together.
5. Mix the milk and vinegar in a measuring jug and let it sit for a few minutes to create a buttermilk substitute.
6. Gradually add the dry ingredients and the buttermilk mixture to the egg mixture, alternating between the two, and mixing until a smooth batter forms.
7. Stir in the melted butter.
8. Pour the batter into the prepared baking dish and smooth the top.
9. Stir the orange zest into the batter before pouring it into the baking dish.
10. For the orange sauce, combine the fresh orange juice, unsalted butter, and granulated sugar in a saucepan. Heat the mixture over low heat until the butter has melted and the sugar has dissolved. Do not boil.
11. When the pudding is done baking, remove it from the oven and immediately pour the hot orange sauce over the hot pudding.
12. Allow the pudding to absorb the sauce for a few minutes before serving.
13. Serve the Orange Malva Pudding warm with a dollop of whipped cream and a slice of fresh orange on the side.

Coffee Malva Pudding

Amarula Malva Pudding

Ingredients:

250g (1 1/4 cups) granulated sugar
2 large eggs
15ml (1 tbsp) smooth apricot jam
200g (1 2/3 cups) all-purpose flour
5ml (1 tsp) baking soda (bicarbonate of soda)
A pinch of salt
30ml (2 tbsp) Amarula liqueur
250ml (1 cup) milk
15ml (1 tbsp) vinegar
30ml (2 tbsp) melted butter

For the Amarula Sauce:
250ml (1 cup) heavy cream
125g (1/2 cup) unsalted butter
125ml (1/2 cup) granulated sugar
125ml (1/2 cup) hot water
30ml (2 tbsp) Amarula liqueur

Instructions:

1. Preheat your oven to 180°C (350°F) and grease a baking dish (approximately 20x20cm or 8x8 inches).
2. In a large mixing bowl, cream together the sugar and eggs until light and fluffy.
3. Add the apricot jam to the egg mixture and beat until well combined.
4. In a separate bowl, sift the flour, baking soda, and salt together.
5. Mix the milk and vinegar in a measuring jug and let it sit for a few minutes to create a buttermilk substitute.
6. Gradually add the dry ingredients and the buttermilk mixture to the egg mixture, alternating between the two, and mixing until a smooth batter forms.
7. Stir in the melted butter.
8. Pour the batter into the prepared baking dish and smooth the top.
9. Stir the Amarula liqueur into the batter before pouring it into the baking dish.
10. For the Amarula sauce, combine the heavy cream, unsalted butter, granulated sugar, hot water, and Amarula liqueur in a saucepan. Heat the mixture over low heat until the butter has melted and the sugar has dissolved. Do not boil.
11. When the pudding is done baking, remove it from the oven and immediately pour the hot Amarula sauce over the hot pudding.
12. Allow the pudding to absorb the sauce for a few minutes before serving.
13. Serve the Amarula Malva Pudding warm with a drizzle of extra Amarula liqueur on top.

Ingredients:

250g (1 1/4 cups) granulated sugar
2 large eggs
15ml (1 tbsp) smooth apricot jam
200g (1 2/3 cups) all-purpose flour
5ml (1 tsp) baking soda (bicarbonate of soda)
A pinch of salt
30ml (2 tbsp) instant coffee granules
250ml (1 cup) milk   *dissolved in 30ml (2 tbsp) hot water*
15ml (1 tbsp) vinegar
30ml (2 tbsp) melted butter

For the Coffee Sauce:
250ml (1 cup) heavy cream
125g (1/2 cup) unsalted butter
125ml (1/2 cup) granulated sugar
125ml (1/2 cup) hot water
15ml (1 tbsp) instant coffee granules
dissolved in 15ml (1 tbsp) hot water

Instructions:

1. Preheat your oven to 180°C (350°F) and grease a baking dish (approximately 20x20cm or 8x8 inches).
2. In a large mixing bowl, cream together the sugar and eggs until light and fluffy.
3. Add the apricot jam to the egg mixture and beat until well combined.
4. In a separate bowl, sift the flour, baking soda, and salt together.
5. Mix the milk and vinegar in a measuring jug and let it sit for a few minutes to create a buttermilk substitute.
6. Gradually add the dry ingredients and the buttermilk mixture to the egg mixture, alternating between the two, and mixing until a smooth batter forms.
7. Stir in the melted butter.
8. Pour the batter into the prepared baking dish and smooth the top.
9. Stir the dissolved coffee granules into the batter before pouring it into the baking dish.
10. For the coffee sauce, combine the heavy cream, unsalted butter, granulated sugar, hot water, and dissolved coffee granules in a saucepan. Heat the mixture over low heat until the butter has melted and the sugar has dissolved. Do not boil.
11. When the pudding is done baking, remove it from the oven and immediately pour the hot coffee sauce over the hot pudding.
12. Allow the pudding to absorb the sauce for a few minutes before serving.
13. Serve the Coffee Malva Pudding warm with a scoop of coffee-flavored ice cream or a dollop of whipped cream.

Enjoy the delightful coffee-infused goodness!

Notes

Notes

SURVIVAL FOOD
South African Pioneer History and Cuisine

Pioneer Boere Recipes were more than just delicious meals; they played a vital role in ensuring food security for families during both prosperous and challenging times. These recipes were developed by the pioneering Boere settlers who ventured into new territories, such as the Great Trek in South Africa between 1835 and 1854.

As these pioneers embarked on their journey, they faced countless hardships and uncertainties. They had to rely on their resourcefulness and ingenuity to sustain themselves and their families. With limited access to markets and provisions, they developed recipes using the ingredients they had readily available, including locally sourced produce, game meat, and preserved goods.

These recipes were carefully crafted to provide nourishment, sustenance, and a sense of comfort in difficult times. They were designed to maximize the use of available resources and make the most out of limited ingredients. Traditional Boere dishes like potjiekos (a slow-cooked stew), biltong (dried meat), and melktert (milk tart) were born out of necessity and practicality, yet they continue to be beloved culinary treasures in South African culture today.

The Pioneer Boere Recipes not only offered sustenance but also helped establish a sense of community and resilience among the settlers. These recipes were passed down through generations, preserving the culinary heritage and connecting families to their pioneering roots.

In times of plenty, these recipes served as a reminder of the perseverance and resilience of the pioneers, and in times of scarcity, they provided a lifeline, ensuring that families had access to nourishing meals even during challenging periods.

Today, Pioneer Boere Recipes serve as a link to our rich history and remind us of the strength and resourcefulness of those who came before us. They continue to be cherished as culinary treasures, providing not only delicious meals but also a connection to our past and a sense of security for our families, both in good times and in bad.

www.ingramcontent.com/pod-product-compliance
Lightning Source LLC
Chambersburg PA
CBRC090826120626
46547CB00008B/617